FORTY WOODEN BOATS

A CATALOG OF BUILDING PLANS
Volume III

By the Editors
of
WoodenBoat Magazine

To Order Boatbuilding Plans, Contact:

The WoodenBoat Store
84 Great Cove Drive
Post Office Box 78
Brooklin, Maine 04616 USA
Tel: 1.800.273.7447 or 207.359.4647
Fax: 207 359.2058
Email: wbstore@woodenboat.com
Order on-line: www.woodenboatstore.com

FORTY WOODEN BOATS
ISBN 10: 0-937822-32-9
ISBN: 13: 978-0-937822-32-6
Printed in the USA by RR Donnelley

WoodenBoat Books, PO Box 78, Brooklin, Maine 04616 USA
www.woodenboatbooks.com

15 14 13 12 11 10 9 8 7 6

A Catalog of Building Plans

WoodenBoat

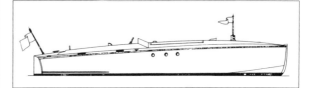

Introduction

This is our third major catalog of boat plans. First published in 1995, it has been back to press several times. We have previously published *Fifty Wooden Boats* (1984) and *Thirty Wooden Boats* (1988) which have also proved popular with readers. Each book has its own unique mix of drawings.

This third volume contains a most eclectic and exciting group of plans: canoes, kayaks, pulling boats, high-performance sliding seat rowing craft, daysailers, cruising sail-boats, and powerboats. You'll find classic and contemporary designs—some drawn by the old masters, and others from the boards of promising young architects.

Construction methods range from simple and quick sheet plywood to traditional plank-on-frame. In between, you'll find drawings for strip-planked hulls, stitch-and-tape kayaks, and glued plywood lapstrake boats. Many of the designs allow you to choose among several optional constructions according to your experience and inclinations.

In his essay "Before You Begin", expert builder and designer Joel White (1930-1997) shows you how to estimate lumber needed to build a boat from the information given in the plans and specifications.

For every boat that hits the water, most of us will launch fifty boats with our imaginations. Dreaming is part of the game. Don't be awed by the enormity of a project. Please, be aware of—but not intimidated by—the necessary commitment. We once asked a sailor if she regretted having spent five years building her offshore cruiser. Her reply: "It would have taken me five years not to build it, too."

Our thanks go to Cynthia Curtis, Doug Hylan, and Mike O'Brien, who compiled this catalog with hopes that you find the words enlightening, the drawings inspiring, and your choices all the more informed.

Before You Begin

A guide to compiling a boatbuilding lumber list

by Joel White

Ordering lumber for a boatbuilding project often seems to be a problem for boatbuilders, whether amateur or professional. Many hesitate when confronted with the need to produce a lumber list from a set of boat plans. It takes some practice to look over the designer's drawings and compile a lumber list, with quantities, from which one can build a boat. Sometimes a set of plans will include a lumber list, but it is always advisable to check it over before ordering. Some builders are not familiar with lumberyard practice and terms, and feel shy about asking a lumber dealer what might seem to be a silly question. Here's how to go about getting the wood you need.

Sources

Let's talk a bit about sources for lumber, before getting into the specifics of ordering. I would break down the sources as follows:

1) Local lumber from local mills.
2) Domestic lumber from local building-supply outlets.
3) Domestic and imported timber from lumber dealers.
4) Other sources—logs cut and milled by you, other people's boatbuilding projects gone sour, drift logs or driftwood, etc.

Any or all of these sources can be used to acquire the wood you need to build your boat. For instance, here in the East, the backbone and the planking material for the boat under construction might be oak and cedar obtained as live-edge (flitch-sawn) stock from your local lumber mill; the molds and ribbands would be built from spruce planks obtained at the nearest building-supply house; and the mast might be a tree cut on your own land behind your house, and four-sided with a chainsaw right in the woods. The mahogany for the stern and cabinsides, to be finished bright, might come from a specialty lumber dealer.

Lumber Nomenclature

Lumberyards and lumber dealers use slightly different language to describe timber than most of us are accustomed to. For instance, thickness is given in quarters of an inch: 1″-thick lumber is called "$\frac{4}{4}$" (said "four-quarter"), 1¼″ lumber is called "$\frac{5}{4}$" (said "five-quarter"), and so on up through $\frac{16}{4}$. Above this thickness, it is more common to talk of 6″ thickness or 8″ thickness. Width of

lumber is normally described in inches, and length in feet. So a piece of timber 1½″ thick by 9″ wide and 12′ long would be written as $\frac{6}{4} \times 9″ \times 12′$.

When buying lumber in some quantity, it is usual to specify the quantity needed in board feet, and to purchase under the designation "RWL" (this stands for "random width and length"). Thus, an order for 200 board feet $\frac{5}{4}$ RWL Honduras mahogany would produce a nice pile of mahogany boards 1¼″ thick, of varying widths and lengths. A board foot of lumber is 1 square foot of timber 1″ thick (or half a square foot 2″ thick).

A word of caution here: Lumber thickness is always given in the rough, just as it comes from the saw. Thus, to get finished (planed on both sides) lumber 1″ thick, you must order $\frac{5}{4}$. Allow a minimum of ¼″ thickness for dressing lumber to its finished thickness. If the lumber is accurately sawn, with little variation in thickness throughout its length, you may be able to do a bit better than this, but you cannot count on it. If you do not have a planer, or access to one, most lumberyards will supply your lumber planed to any thickness you specify, but you will be paying for the rough thickness from which it was milled, plus a fee for the milling.

Another thing to remember: Your building-supply outlet will deal mostly in dimensioned lumber— like 2 × 4s, 2 × 10s, etc., which will actually measure 1½ × 3½″ and 1½ × 9½″, respectively. Length of dimensioned lumber is in even numbers of feet—8′, 10′, 12′, 14′, 16′. So, try to adjust your order to accommodate these dimensions. Many building-supply outfits, however, will supply lumber sawn to your specifications.

Species

The sawmill or lumber dealer will need to know what species of tree you seek. Mostly, this is straightforward. White oak, Northern white cedar, Southern cedar (often called Virginia white cedar), ash, cypress, Eastern white pine, Sitka spruce, teak, and the many varieties of mahogany will be carried by a well-stocked lumberyard, plus a number of other species not generally known as boatbuilding woods. Some timbers will be domestic; others are imported. Most boats are built using some of each. As a general rule, imported lumber will be higher priced than domestic, but

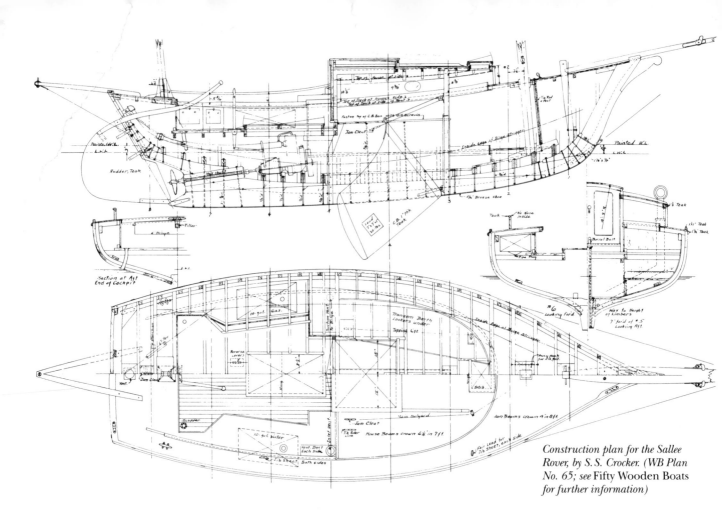

Construction plan for the Sallee Rover, by S. S. Crocker. (WB Plan No. 65; see Fifty Wooden Boats *for further information)*

demand and availability really determine the price.

Confusion may arise when there are several names given to the same species. An example is yellow cedar and Alaska cedar; as far as I know, this is the same tree with two different names. Hackmatack is often called "tamarack" or "larch," and there are a dozen or more different species that are all sawn into "Philippine mahogany." If you are going to use Philippine mahogany, specify "dark."

Grade

Trying to understand the grading of lumber for quality leads to a real morass of terms, and standards seem to vary from company to company, country to country. Rather than get both of us into an area of confusion, my advice to you is to find a lumber dealer you can talk to, tell him what you are trying to build, what is needed for quality, and he will tell you what he has and how much it will cost. Most lumber dealers who handle boat timber are aware of the quality needed and try to stock such timber. I find it helpful to explain how the material will be used. If you need clear white oak for steam-bending frames, specify that it come from clear, straight-grained butt logs. Honduras mahogany often can be had in either straight-grained or more heavily figured stock. The wild-grained lumber may make a handsomer cabin table, but the straight-grained will be better for planking.

It is sometimes possible to specify whether you want flat or vertical grain. Another variable which enters into the quality of your lumber is its dryness, or lack thereof.

Most lumber obtained from a specialty lumber dealer will be dry, often kiln-dried. Some outfits handle both air-dried and kiln-dried timber. In general, air-dried is preferable for boatbuilding use. If you go to your neighborhood sawmill and order material sawn from the log, it will be pretty green. For the backbone stock, this is perfectly satisfactory. These items will be, for the most part, underwater, and will swell and shrink less if green rather than dry. In truth, it is not feasible to completely dry large oak timbers. Trying to do so would only result in the timbers twisting and checking to such a degree that they would become unusable. A couple of coats of red lead on the backbone structure after assembly will prevent the green oak from drying and checking too much while the boat is under construction. Planking stock, on the other hand, should be obtained far enough in advance of building to allow it to be well air dried before use.

Plywood

You may or may not use some plywood in your boatbuilding project. Here are a few facts that will help when ordering plywood. The standard panel size, even for imported plywood, is $4 \times 8'$; sometimes $10'$ panels are available on a limited basis. If you must have longer sheets, these can be ordered custom scarfed, or you can do it yourself. Standard thicknesses are ¼", ⅜", ½", and ¾"; other thicknesses, both thinner and thicker, are sometimes available. The test of quality in plywood is the number of plies, and the absence of interior voids. A high-quality ¼" panel

Joel White

Figure 1: *Laying out patterns for the stem, stem knee, and gammon knee on a peice of 5" × 10' oak stock.*

will have five plies, a less-good panel only three. The best ¾" panels will have thirteen plies, a less-good panel only seven. I would recommend using only marine-grade plywood, as exterior grades contain an unacceptable number of voids. Any void is unacceptable, except for cabin joinerwork, and if the edge-grain of the plywood is to show, voids won't do there, either. Most foreign plywood is measured for thickness in millimeters (6mm is just under ¼", 9mm just under ⅜", 12mm just under ½", and 18mm just less than ¾"). High-quality panels should have all plies of equal thickness. Sometimes you see plywood with thick core plies and thin face veneers; avoid these, except perhaps for cabin furniture. Quality of the face veneers is designated as A, B, C, or D, A being the highest and D the lowest. Thus, an "AA" designation means both face veneers are of best quality, while "AC" or "AD" means one good face, and the other not so good. Some large lumber dealers handle marine plywood, some do not. There are a number of companies that deal only in plywood panels, and these companies usually have the largest inventories and the best selection of panels.

Estimating Quantity

We will now go through the process of making up the lumber list needed to build a boat. Let's use as an example the nice little S.S. Crocker design No. 300, a 20' overall centerboard sloop (or yawl). More than 20 years ago I built one of these dandy little boats, so I happen to have the plans and specifications on hand, and some remembrance of what is needed for materials.

Backbone

Start your list with the pieces needed for the vessel's backbone. These usually are the biggest pieces of timber in the boat. Crocker's specification for the backbone reads "of oak or African mahogany, sided as per rabbet, molded as shown." Let's choose white oak as the material for the backbone. If you can find a local mill that is sawing white oak logs, this is probably your best bet to get the heavy backbone stock. Specify that it be sawn live edge, with the bark and sapwood left on the edges. You must tell the mill operator the thickness of each piece required, the minimum width (clear of sapwood) needed to get out the part involved, and the length of each piece. For example: If you have already lofted the backbone full-size, you can measure the size of the keel directly from your patterns. If the lofting isn't done yet, referring to the plans will show that the keel scales to be 14' long, with a maximum siding of 7½" and a greatest molded depth (near amidships) of 8". It tapers toward the ends in both siding and molding. In order to have a bit of extra wood to allow for defects and sweeps in a big piece such as this, it would be advis-

able to order a piece of oak 8 × 9". Because large timbers often have checks in the ends, I would order a piece 16' long, so that some can be cut from each end.

Bolted to the forward end of the main keel are four more pieces of backbone: the forefoot (or "gripe"), the stem, the knee that joins the two, and a small gammon knee. The stem and stem knee have a finished siding of 4½" and thus must be ordered from 5" stock. The stem is about 5' long and has a maximum width (molding) of 9". Both the stem knee and the gammon knee are about 2' long. So, order a piece of 5" × 9" × 10' long oak, figuring to get the stem from the best part of it, and the two knees from the remainder. Figure 1 shows patterns for these three pieces laid out on the oak. The forefoot, which runs aft to Station 3, must be gotten from thicker stock, because at Station 3 the keel rabbet has swelled to a width of nearly 7". It is 5½' long and molds 7". Sawmills don't like to saw

Figure 2: *Accommodating the concave curve in the horn timber.*

really short pieces of timber (6' or less), so try to get two or more short backbone pieces out of one larger piece of timber. Pursuing this idea, notice that the after deadwood (between the main keel and the shaftlog) is sided 7¼", molded 6", and is also about 5½' long. So, let's plan to saw both these parts, the after deadwood and the forefoot, from a baulk of timber of 7½" × 8" × 12'. To complete our backbone timbers, we need the shaftlog, the horn timber, and a small stern knee. Scaling from the lines and construction plan or measuring the full-sized lofting (if completed) will show us that one more piece of timber 7" thick, 8" wide, and 8' long will enable us to get out these three pieces. Note that the horn timber is concave on its upper side. Figure 2 shows how this curve must be bridged when measuring for the molded width that you must order. Don't try to be too cute when ordering backbone material—buy a little more than you need, rather than just enough. If you have been generous in size with the stock ordered, it will be easier to avoid the inevitable small defects found in any piece of timber. Check the plans for other heavy timbers needed. Are there any mooring bitts, pawl posts, quarter bitts, or maststeps shown on the plans that must come from heavy timbers? If so, include them in your order of backbone material.

On the little Crocker sloop, there are two more items which need to come out of fairly heavy stock: the centerboard trunk logs and the mooring bitt. The bitt is 3 × 3" oak 3½' long, the two trunk logs each 3 × 4" and 5' long.

Continued on page 80

17'1" B. N. Morris Canoe

plans by Rollin Thurlow

PARTICULARS

LOA	17'1"
Beam	33"
Weight	
(wood-canvas)	85 lbs
(wood-strip-plank)	95 lbs
(wood-strip-fiberglass)	85 lbs

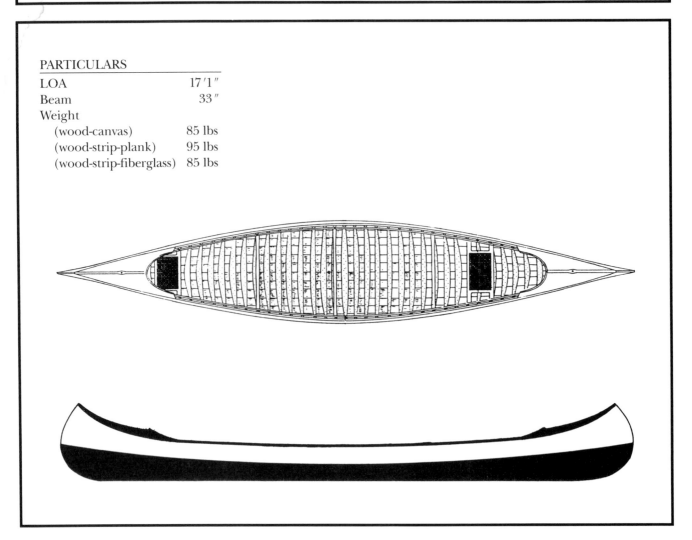

Designer/builder Rollin Thurlow took the lines shown here from a surviving 17' B.N. Morris canoe (Model A-64, Type 3) that had been built in 1908. According to the builder's catalog, the Model A combined "the most important features that are required in an all-round canoe...great stability, good speed, good paddling qualities, together with a remarkable carrying capacity on slight draught." "Type 3" indicated that this canoe had longer decks and other details that marked it as being top of the line.

Paddlers with salt water in their veins might question this design—and, for that matter, most other "Indian" or Canadian canoes. Look at all that tumblehome (the sides curve toward the boat's centerline as they near the rails). Won't it invite green water aboard, and won't it reduce secondary stability? And what about the seats located high up in the ends of the boat? Doesn't this arrangement put the paddlers' weight up where it shouldn't be for rough-water work? The answer to all of the above is, "Yes, but...."

Tumblehome keeps the rails clear of the paddlers' knuckles, and this allows more efficient strokes. Also, the hull tends to be structurally stiffer because it approaches the tubular configuration of a decked canoe. As for the seats, their height permits more powerful strokes. And their far forward and aft locations provide better steering.

This historic Morris canoe will carry a larger load than any comparable decked competitor, and it will do so while giving sharp control in shallow and tight streams. Most necessary repairs can be made with materials at hand. Used in its native inland Maine waters for its intended purposes, old Model A-64, Type 3 seems to approach perfection.

Thurlow's beautifully detailed drawings describe three different construction methods for this canoe: traditional wood-and-canvas; all-wood strip-on-frame; and wood-strip fiberglass. Plans consist of eight sheets and include full-sized mold patterns and construction details for each canoe, as well as lines and offsets for the wood-and-canvas and all-wood strip-on-frame versions. WB Plan No. 96, $60.00.

Plan 96

DESCRIPTION
Hull type: Round-bottomed Indian-type canoe
Construction: wood-canvas, wood-strip-plank, or
  wood-strip fiberglass

PERFORMANCE
*Suitable for: Protected waters
*Intended capacity: 1–3
  Trailerable or cartoppable
  Propulsion: Paddle, pole

BUILDING DATA
Skill needed: Intermediate
Lofting required: No
*Alternative construction: As described

PLANS DATA
No. of sheets: 8
Level of detail: Above average
Cost per set: $60.00
WB Plan No. 96

See page 96 for further information.

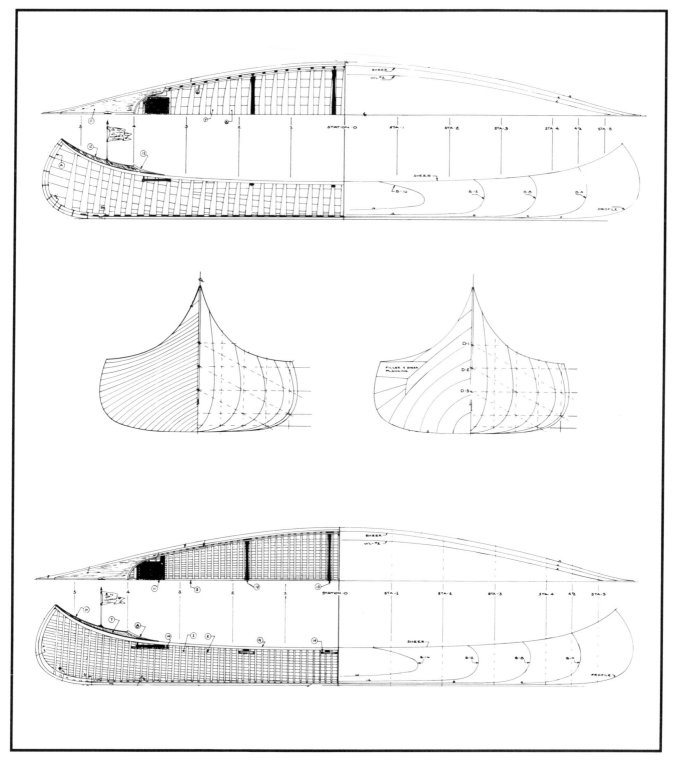

16'7" Skimalong II Kayak

by Paul Ford

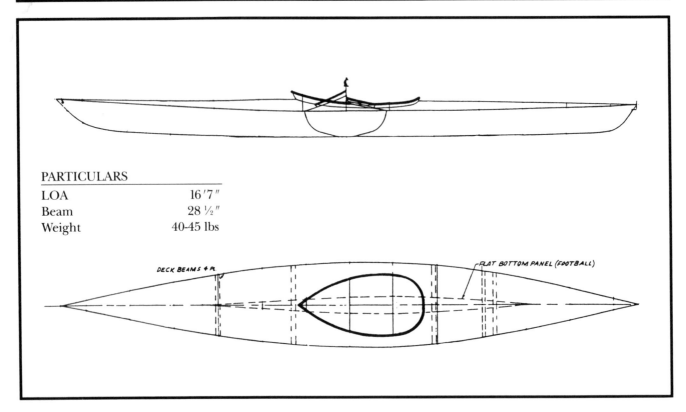

PARTICULARS

LOA	16'7"
Beam	28 ½"
Weight	40-45 lbs

DECK BEAMS 4 R.   FLAT BOTTOM PANEL (FOOTBALL)

Skimalong's beautiful strip-built hull combines grace, speed, and stability. With a substantial beam of 28 ½" (24 ½" at the waterline), this boat allows paddlers to re-enter the cockpit from deep water without the aid of paddle-floats or other special gear (the colder the water, the faster the re-entry). Yet the round-bilged hull paddles as easily as many narrower hulls of cruder form.

The 42"-long cockpit allows plenty of room for bending your knees, sitting cross-legged, or settling down for a nap after lunch. And it is designed to keep paddle drip on deck, not in your lap. All of this amounts to comfortable and relaxed paddling.

The strip-built hull will require more time to build than will sheet-plywood kayaks; but you'll be working with small, inexpensive, easily handled pieces of wood. You'll not lose sleep worrying about cutting into $200 sheets of imported plywood, and the overall materials cost can be less than for plywood boats. Everything aboard Skimalong is held together with epoxy and fiberglass. No metal fastenings are needed.

Skimalong is a lightweight, comfortable, easily driven, roomy kayak for day paddling and for extended trips along the coast. It tracks well yet turns readily. And you'll be proud of its fine appearance.

Skimalong's four sheets of plans include: general layout and construction; full-sized patterns for molds, deck forms, bow and stern; and a 10-page instruction booklet. WB Plan No. 114, $45.00.

Plan 114

DESCRIPTION
Hull type: Round-bottomed sea kayak
Construction: Strip planked
PERFORMANCE
*Suitable for: Protected waters
*Intended capacity: 1
  Trailerable or cartoppable
  Propulsion: Double paddle

BUILDING DATA
Skill needed: Basic to intermediate
Lofting required: Yes
*Alternative construction: None
PLANS DATA
No. of sheets: 4 plus instruction booklet
Level of detail: Above average
Cost per set: $45.00
WB Plan No. 114

See page 96 for further information.

17'10" Seguin Kayak

by Rob Bryan

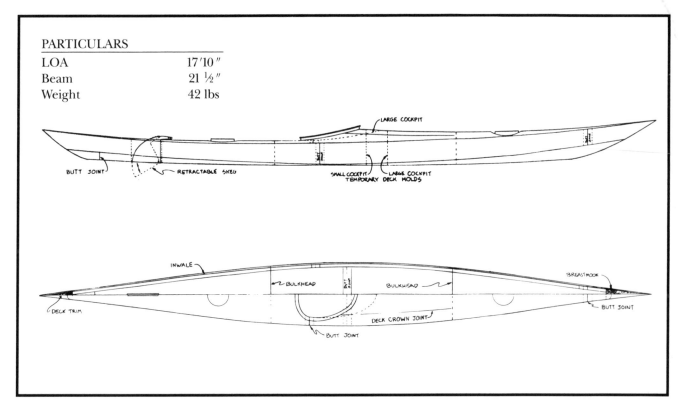

PARTICULARS

LOA	17'10"
Beam	21 ½"
Weight	42 lbs

Seguin, a sports car of a kayak, will reward experienced paddlers with spirited performance.

Designer Rob Bryan has added a retractable skeg to this kayak to assure positive control without the complication of a rudder system. Spectators watching sea kayaks working into big waves often comment on the daring of the paddlers. In fact, blasting to windward is the easiest part of rough-water kayaking in terms of the skills required. Sea kayaks, with their low profiles and pointed noses, love that game. The real test of operator ability occurs when paddling across, or off, the wind. Some kayaks tend to dig in and root when traveling with wind and wave. Many kayaks want to round up and face into the wind, no matter where the paddler might want to go. By raising or lowering Seguin's skeg, you can head where you wish at will.

With Seguin's cockpit tailored to your own dimensions (using specially shaped foam pads), this kayak becomes an extension of your body. You'll be able to lean, brace, and Eskimo roll with great ease and style.

Despite all its sophistication, Seguin is easy to build. Simply cut the hull panels to shape, stitch them together, and finish the seams with epoxy and fiberglass tape. This is a clean, light (42 lbs), and strong boat. And it is extraordinarily handsome on the water.

Plans include profile, deck plan, and panel layout; three sheets of construction details; full-sized patterns for skeg and cockpit; and a 40-page construction manual. WB Plan No. 111, $60.00.

Plan 111

DESCRIPTION
Hull type: V-bottomed sea kayak
Construction: Stitch-and-glue plywood
Featured in WB No. 115
PERFORMANCE
*Suitable for: Protected waters
*Intended capacity: 1
Trailerable or cartoppable
Propulsion: Double paddle

BUILDING DATA
Skill needed: Basic to intermediate
Lofting required: No
*Alternative construction: None
PLANS DATA
No. of sheets: 5 plus instruction booklet
Level of detail: Above average
Cost per set: $60.00
WB Plan No. 111

*See page 96 for further information.

17' and 18' Cape Charles Kayaks

by Chris Kulczycki

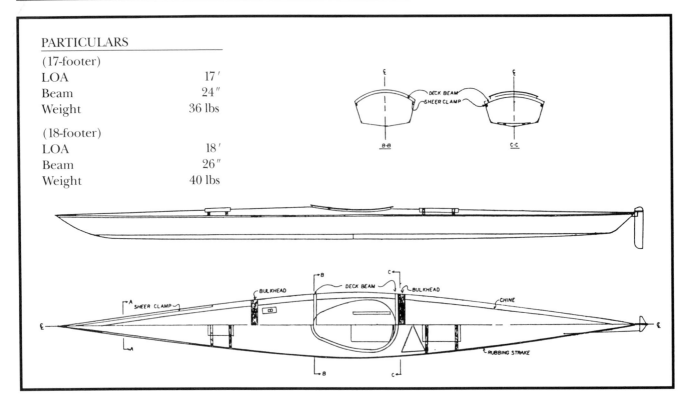

PARTICULARS

(17-footer)
LOA	17'
Beam	24"
Weight	36 lbs

(18-footer)
LOA	18'
Beam	26"
Weight	40 lbs

The Cape Charles 17 is a versatile touring kayak. It will hold a 180-lb paddler and a week's worth of gear, yet it tracks well with a 140-lb paddler and no gear. On the other hand, designer Chris Kulczycki drew the Cape Charles 18 for serious long-distance travel. This is a big kayak that can handle 250-lb paddlers and expedition-sized cargoes. Both kayaks are built using the easy stitch-and-glue technique. Simply cut the plywood panels to shape, stitch them together, and secure the seams with fiberglass tape and epoxy. Weighing only 36 lbs and 40 lbs respectively, the Cape Charles 17 and 18 are considerably lighter than their store-bought equivalents.

These kayaks can be finished without hatches and rudders (a fashion favored by many experienced pad-dlers—including countless generations of Inuit experts). Or you can add all the bells and whistles that are touted by contemporary purveyors of sea kayaks. If you are willing to invest the time needed to become a capable kayaker, we suggest adhering to the simple outfitting that has served paddlers for more than 5,000 years—gear that doesn't exist cannot break, weighs not a single ounce, and costs not a penny.

Plans for the Cape Charles kayaks include: profile and deck plans; patterns for bow and stern; plank layouts; patterns for hatches, coamings, and backrests; and 26-page instruction booklets. WB Plan Nos. 117 (17-footer) and 118 (18-footer).

Plans 117 and 118

DESCRIPTION
Hull type: V-bottomed sea kayak
Construction: Stitch-and-glue plywood
PERFORMANCE
*Suitable for: Protected waters
*Intended capacity: 1
Trailerable or cartoppable
Propulsion: Double paddle
BUILDING DATA
Skill needed: Basic to intermediate

Lofting required: No
*Alternative construction: None
Helpful information: "Building the Cape Charles," Pts. 1 and 2, WB Nos. 113 and 114; or *The Kayak Shop* by Chris Kulczycki
PLANS DATA
No. of sheets: 4 plus instruction booklet
Level of detail: Above average

WB Plan Nos. 117 (17-footer) and 118 (18-footer)
These plans are no longer available for purchase.

21' Tred Avon Kayak

by Chris Kulczycki

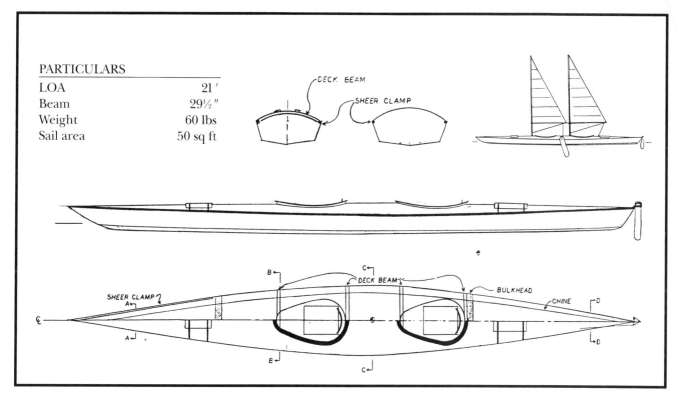

PARTICULARS

LOA	21'
Beam	29½"
Weight	60 lbs
Sail area	50 sq ft

Tred Avon is an able 60-lb cruiser that will take two people almost anywhere along the coast. Although many paddlers prefer taking their pleasure in single kayaks, double kayaks offer advantages that make them valuable additions to any fleet. They allow partners of vastly different capabilities to travel together without boring the stronger or terrifying the weaker. Compared to single kayaks, doubles are usually more stable, often faster, and almost always less expensive per paddler.

Designer Chris Kulczycki drew the 21'x 29½" Tred Avon as a big brother for his 18' Cape Charles single kayak. The boats show a strong family resemblance: relatively flat sheerlines (for easy construction and low windage); moderate deadrise and rocker (to reduce wetted surface for easier propulsion, and to provide better handling in rough water); stitch-and-glue plywood/epoxy construction (for fast building and a stiff, light hull).

This kayak's cockpits are positioned close to each other. The benefits of this configuration include more comfortable conversation and better weight distribution for rough-water work (the ends of the boat can be kept light, allowing the kayak to rise more easily to the waves).

Tred Avon's plans include: profile, sail plan, deck plan; patterns for bow and stern; plank layout; patterns for hatches, coaming, and back rest; deck frames and a large cockpit option; and a 26-page instruction booklet. WB Plan. No. 115.

Plan 115

DESCRIPTION
Hull type: V-bottomed sea kayak
Rig: Cat schooner
Construction: Stitch-and-glue plywood
PERFORMANCE
*Suitable for: Protected waters
*Intended capacity: 2
Trailerable or cartoppable
Propulsion: Double paddle
BUILDING DATA
Skill needed: Basic to intermediate

Lofting required: No
*Alternative construction: None
Helpful information: "Building the Cape Charles," Pts. 1 and 2, WB Nos. 113 and 114; or *The Kayak Shop* by Chris Kulczycki
PLANS DATA
No. of sheets: 4 plus instruction booklet
Level of detail: Above average

WB Plan No. 115

These plans are no longer available for purchase.

11'2" Shellback Dinghy

by Joel White

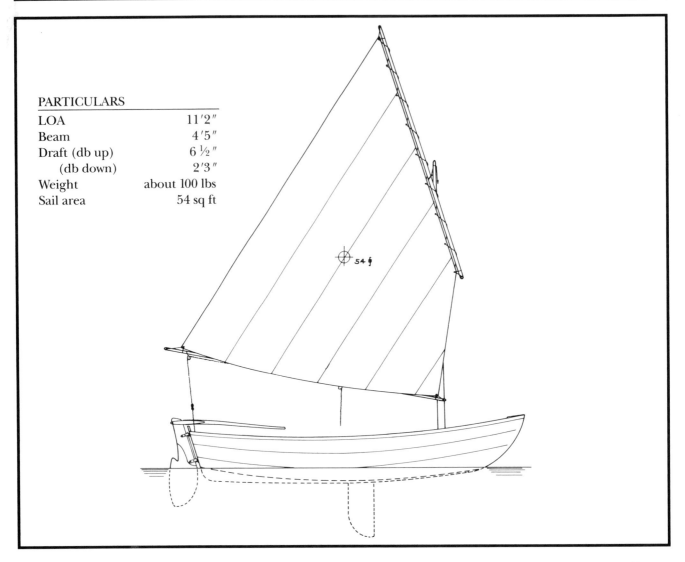

PARTICULARS

LOA	11'2"
Beam	4'5"
Draft (db up)	6 ½"
(db down)	2'3"
Weight	about 100 lbs
Sail area	54 sq ft

It would be hard to imagine a better all-around small boat than the Shellback Dinghy. She is a pleasure to row, and fast and responsive under sail. She is easy to build and maintain, docile and well mannered under tow, small enough to handle easily but big enough to carry a good load. And, she looks great—handsome with just paint, or lovely with a little varnish.

What designer Joel White did for the pram with his terrific Nutshell design, he has done again for larger dinghies with the Shellback. Here is a boat that is elegant of line, can be built by the beginner, and will outperform just about any production dinghy on the market. Scores of these fine boats are already improving the waterfront scene, and you might even be able to find (or start) some hotly contested Shellback racing in your area.

The more experienced builder will have no trouble building Shellback from the plans alone, but for the beginner there is lots of help. First, there's the 53-page monograph *How to*

Build the Shellback Dinghy. The Shellback Model Kit ($79.95) will help you sharpen your boatbuilding skills on a smaller scale. And, complete boat kits are available: $1,295.00 for the rowing version; $1,495.00 if you want to sail as well.

As a teaching tool, the Shellback provides an education in the fine points of sailing, rowing, and sculling for sailors of all ages, her standing lug rig easily dropped altogether if the winds come on too strong. She is not easily adapted to outboard power, primarily because the weight of the motor throws her fine hull out of trim, but she rows well enough to provide plenty of efficiency and speed, even with a load. She is distinctive enough in appearance to attract admiration at every turn, a unique blend of traditional design and modern wood construction.

Shellback's plans come on six sheets and include lines, construction, building jig, plank layouts, and full-sized patterns for molds and other parts. WB Plan No. 109, $75.00.

Plan 109

DESCRIPTION
Hull type: Multi-chine/lapstrake dory-skiff
Rig: Standing lug
Construction: Glued-lapstrake plywood

PERFORMANCE
*Suitable for: Protected waters
*Intended capacity: 1–3
Trailerable or cartoppable
Propulsion: Sail, oars

BUILDING DATA
Skill needed: Basic to intermediate

Lofting required: No
*Alternative construction: Traditional lapstrake
"How to Build" instructions: WB Nos. 116–118 or
How to Build the Shellback Dinghy

PLANS DATA
No. of sheets: 6
Level of detail: Above average
Cost per set: $75.00
WB Plan No. 109

See page 96 for further information.

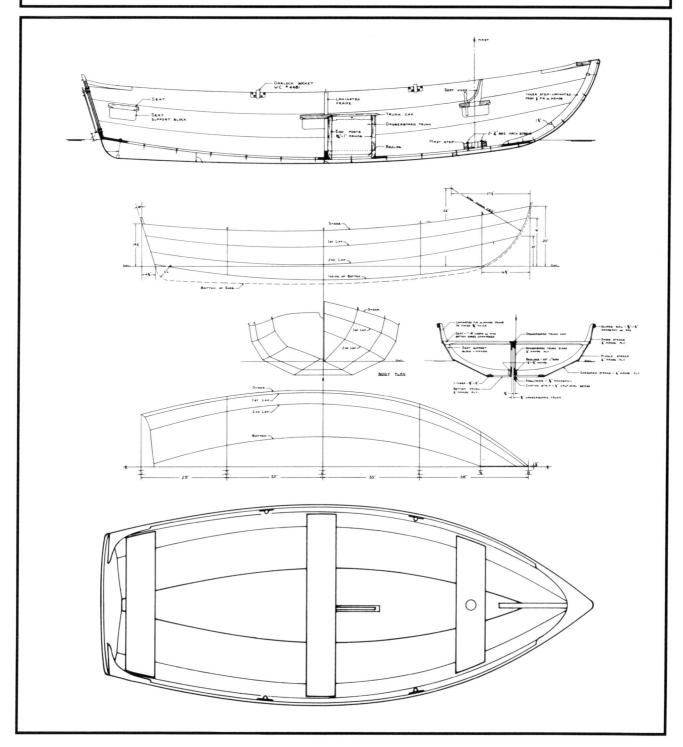

12'10" Pooduck Skiff

by Joel White

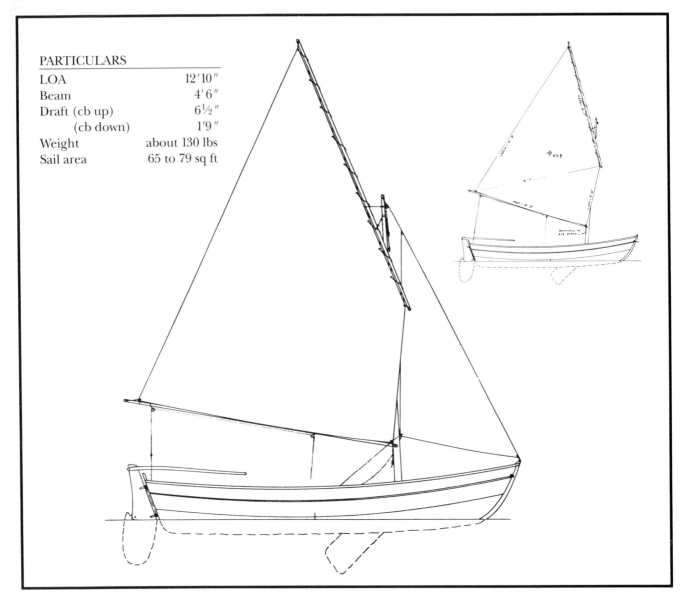

PARTICULARS

LOA	12'10"
Beam	4'6"
Draft (cb up)	6½"
(cb down)	1'9"
Weight	about 130 lbs
Sail area	65 to 79 sq ft

It's a pity that so many people seem to think a dinghy should be a tiny boat. A bigger boat will almost always be easier and faster to row, carry a bigger load, and be more seaworthy. Of course, this holds true for any small boat: bigger is usually better, up to a point. For most small-boat users, that point comes when two people can no longer lug the boat around.

Joel White's Pooduck Skiff is a big little boat—about as large as two average people would want to carry on shore. As a big sister to the 11'2" Shellback Dinghy, she has a lot of the same great qualities: excellent rowing and sailing ability, easy construction, and mannerly towing habits. But you'll be surprised at how much bigger she is. At 12'10" LOA with 4'6" beam, she'll easily carry an extra person or two, and when the weather looks ques-

tionable you'll be glad for her extra size. Her scantlings are ruggedly reassuring as well—she'll be able to take her share of knocks.

As befits her big-sister status, Pooduck sports a grown-up rig: at the captain's discretion, a jib can be added to her lug rig, to provide a little extra speed or just to keep the crew happily busy.

The first-time builder, can, with some effort, make a fine boat from these very complete plans. If a little extra guidance is desired, the 53-page monograph *How to Build the Shellback Dinghy* will prove almost as helpful for Pooduck as for her little sister.

Plans are printed on six sheets, including lines, construction, full-sized patterns for molds, stem and transom, and plank layouts. WB Plan No. 102, $75.00.

Plan 102

DESCRIPTION
Hull type: Multi-chine/lapstrake dory-skiff
Rig: Standing lug
Construction: Glued-lapstrake plywood

PERFORMANCE
*Suitable for: Protected waters
*Intended capacity: 1–4
Trailerable: Yes
Propulsion: Sail, oars

BUILDING DATA
Skill needed: Basic to intermediate

Lofting required: No
Helpful information: *How to Build the Shellback Dinghy*
*Alternative construction: Traditional lapstrake

PLANS DATA
No. of sheets: 6
Level of detail: Above average
Cost per set: $75.00
WB Plan No. 102

See page 96 for further information.

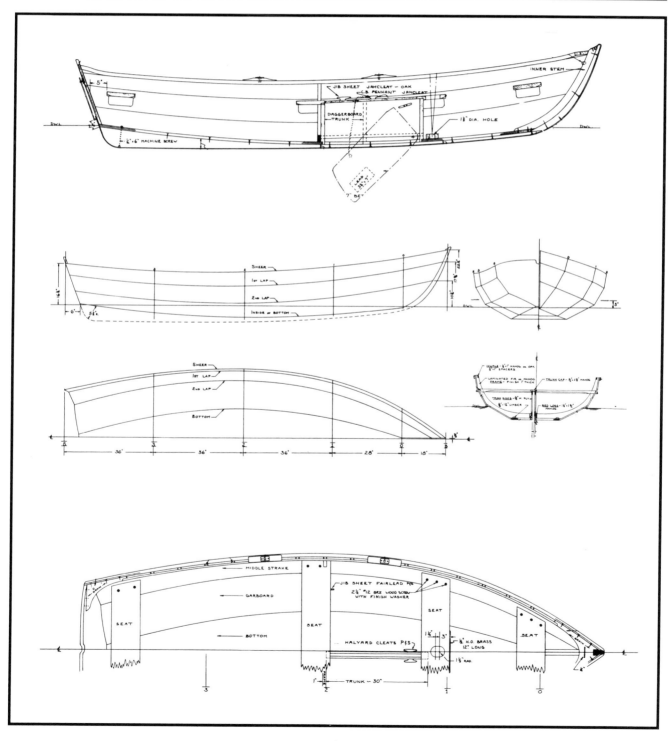

13' Beach Pea Peapod

by Doug Hylan

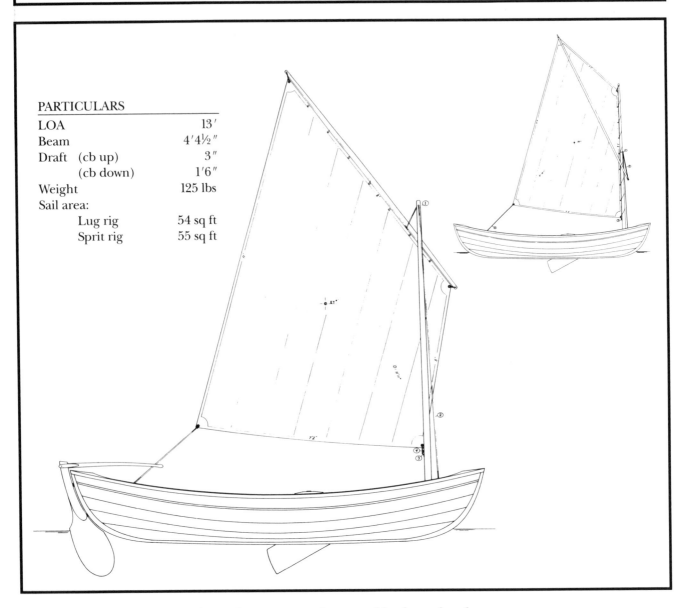

PARTICULARS

LOA	13'
Beam	4'4½"
Draft (cb up)	3"
(cb down)	1'6"
Weight	125 lbs
Sail area:	
Lug rig	54 sq ft
Sprit rig	55 sq ft

Most boats produced as tenders today row so poorly that it is little wonder that their owners often turn to an outboard motor for help. But if you are willing to forgo the noise, expense, and pollution of a motor, you may find that a peapod is the ultimate yacht tender. These are great little boats, seaworthy, stable, and easily rowed. Here is a pod that is a bit smaller than most, but she will still carry a big load and bring you through some lumpy water with confidence.

Beach Pea uses modern glued-lapstrake plywood construction, so she is lighter and easier to build than a traditionally built boat. In addition, you won't have to worry about her seams opening if your pod has been out of the water for a while. The clean interior will be easier to maintain, and a coat of paint will last quite a bit longer on the stable plywood surface.

Two sailing rigs are shown—an easy-to-strike lugsail, and the more traditional sprit rig. Sailing your pod can be a lot of fun, especially if you are willing to go rudderless. Unlikely as this may sound, you can amaze your friends and steer your pod just by moving your weight forward or aft. A centerboard will help you get to windward, and for the less adventurous the plans include a rudder.

Doug Hylan drew Beach Pea's plans with the beginning builder in mind. The plans are well detailed, and full-sized patterns eliminate the need for lofting. The six-sheet set of plans includes lines, construction, two sail plans, and full-sized patterns for molds and stems. A 22-page how-to-build booklet will help you along. WB Plan No. 110, $75.00.

Plan 110

DESCRIPTION
Hull type: Round-bottomed, double-ender
Rig: Lug or sprit rigged
Construction: Glued-lapstrake plywood

PERFORMANCE
*Suitable for: Protected waters
*Intended capacity: 1–4
Trailerable: Yes
Propulsion: Sail, oars

BUILDING DATA
Skill needed: Basic to intermediate
Lofting required: No
*Alternative construction: Traditional lapstrake

PLANS DATA
No. of sheets: 6
Level of detail: Above average
Cost per set: $75.00
WB Plan No. 110

See page 96 for further information.

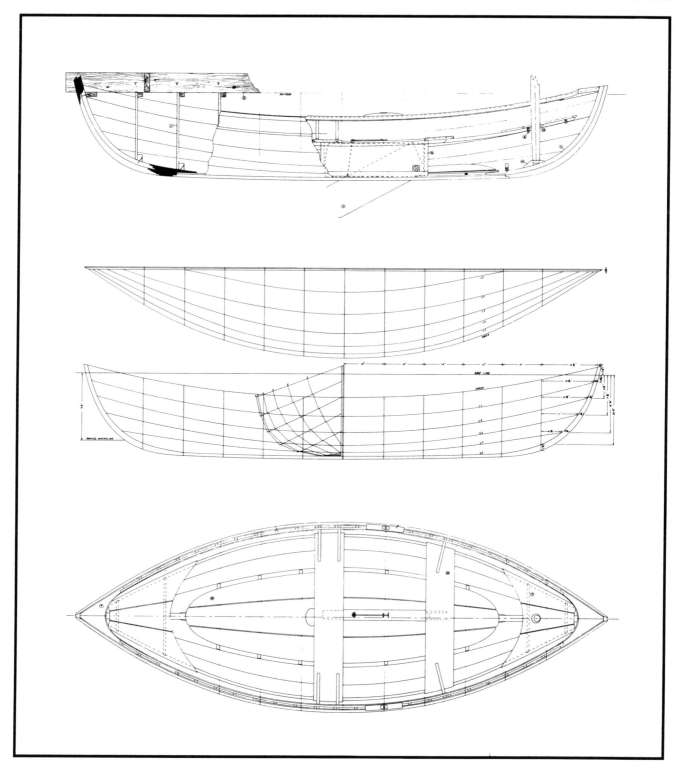

13'9" Skiff, Willy Winship

by John Atkin

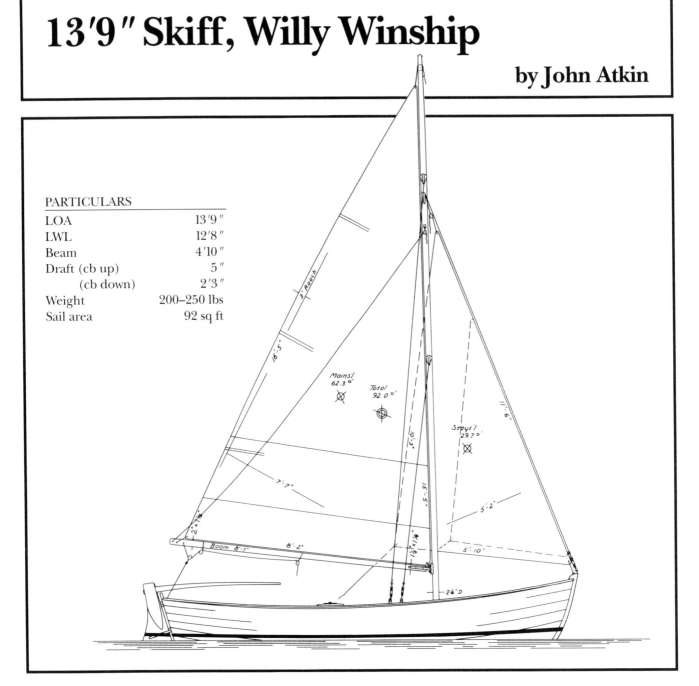

PARTICULARS

LOA	13'9"
LWL	12'8"
Beam	4'10"
Draft (cb up)	5"
(cb down)	2'3"
Weight	200–250 lbs
Sail area	92 sq ft

For many years, William Atkin, later aided by his son John, would turn out a design nearly every month for the readers of *Motor Boating* magazine. These were not just quick sketches but fully developed plans, complete with construction drawings, instructions for the builder, and a bit of history and philosophy thrown in for good measure. Perhaps as remarkable as this prodigious output, was the Atkin ability to come up with a name for each design—some little moniker that would fit with the nature of the boat and stick in the reader's mind. These designs covered craft of every description, but included many small flat-bottomed skiffs for oar, sail, and motor, and it is unlikely that there is any name more associated with the type than Atkin.

Willy Winship was designed by John Atkin and named for a lad of buoyant temperament and high energy, an art student of John's wife, Pat. With its good-sized sail plan

and well-stayed hollow mast, this is a boat conceived primarily for sailing. The oarlocks are there to get you home if the wind dies.

Construction should be well within the abilities of anyone with a bit of woodworking experience and some stick-to-it energy. The plans show two construction methods—traditional solid wood with a cross-planked bottom for those who dislike glue, or a plywood bottom and single-panel plywood topsides for those in a hurry. Or, for a plywood boat with better looks, you could use glued plywood lapping strakes for the topsides. Simple lofting is required but shouldn't be more than a morning's work and would be a good first introduction to the process.

Plans are printed on four sheets, including lines, traditional and plywood construction, arrangements, and sail plan. WB Plan No. 131, $60.00.

Plan 131

DESCRIPTION
Hull type: Flat-bottomed skiff
Rig: Sloop
Construction: Cross-planked bottom, lapstrake sides

PERFORMANCE
*Suitable for: Protected waters
*Intended capacity: 1–4
Trailerable: Yes
Propulsion: Sail, oars

BUILDING DATA
Skill needed: Basic to intermediate
Lofting required: Yes
*Alternative construction: Plywood, glued-lapstrake
  plywood

PLANS DATA
No. of sheets: 4
Level of detail: Average
Cost per set: $60.00
WB Plan No. 131

*See page 96 for further information.

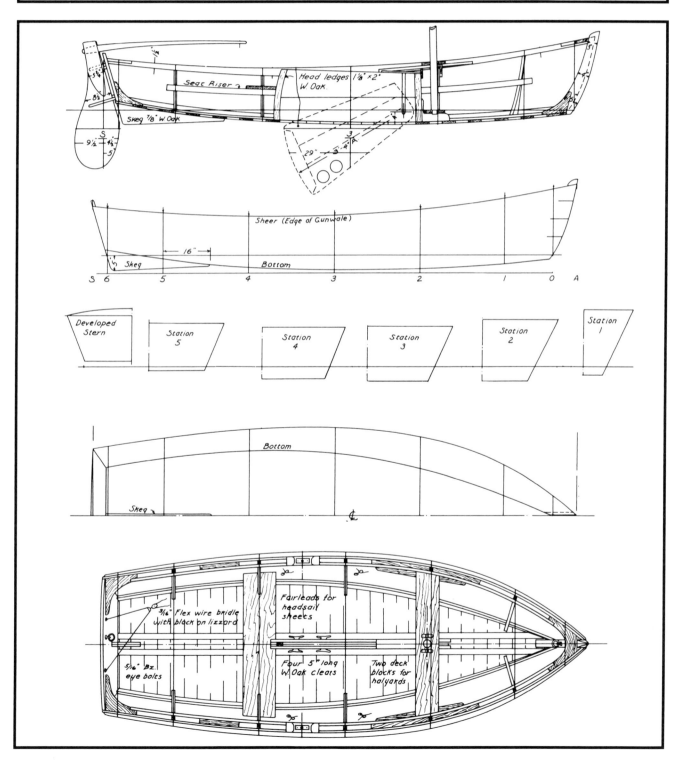

—21—

14′ Maine Coast Peapod

by Joel White

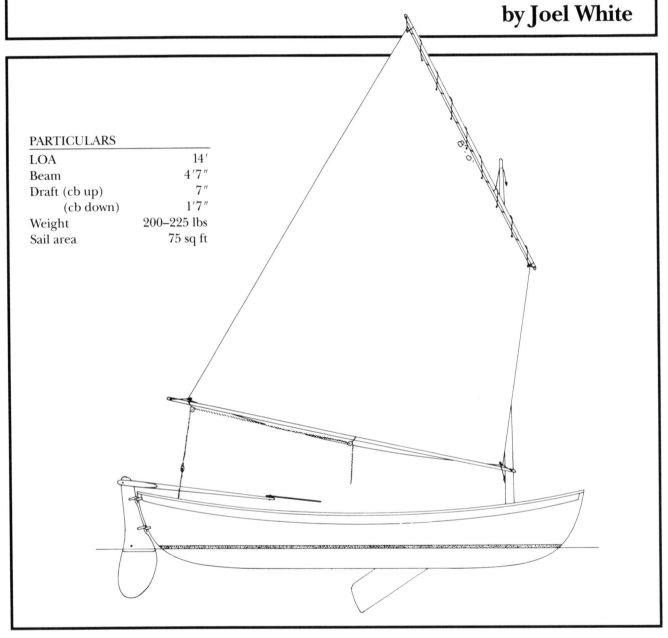

PARTICULARS	
LOA	14′
Beam	4′7″
Draft (cb up)	7″
(cb down)	1′7″
Weight	200–225 lbs
Sail area	75 sq ft

Peapods, which evolved as inshore working boats, were seen all along the Maine coast at the turn of the century. Used for lobstering, clamming, and all kinds of waterfront work, the original boats were usually 14′ to 16′ long and a bit flatter floored and straighter sided than most recreational peapods you'll see today. This made them burdensome and stiff, but even heavily loaded they would row easily. And seaworthy! A good peapod was comfortable in conditions that would make you wish you were close to shore were you in another type of boat.

Joel White's lovely Maine Coast Peapod incorporates the best of these traditional properties. She will carry a big load and row easily, and is as seaworthy as a small open boat can be. Her construction is as traditional as her lines: sweet-smelling ½″ cedar planking over steam-bent oak frames, all fastened together with good, honest bronze and copper. While not simple to build, this would be a great first project for someone interested in learning traditional boatbuilding techniques. She'll be as fun to build as to use and when you step aboard your finished pod, you'll know you've got a real boat under you—stable and solid.

The standard lug rig, while not traditional for peapods, provides plenty of low-cost power. It is easy to make and sail; and the spars stow completely within the boat when not in use. The mast is unstayed—no standing rigging to kink, tangle, or snap. As a bonus, this boat can be rigged to sail in about two minutes.

Plans consist of four sheets: lines, construction, lug rig sail plan, and full-sized patterns for molds, stems, and belt frames. No lofting is required. WB Plan No. 94, $60.00.

Plan 94

DESCRIPTION
Hull type: Round-bottomed double-ender
Rig: Standing lug
Construction: Carvel-planked over steamed frames
PERFORMANCE
*Suitable for: Protected waters
*Intended capacity: 1–4
Trailerable: Yes
Propulsion: Sail, oars

BUILDING DATA
Skill needed: Intermediate
Lofting required: No
*Alternative construction: Lapstrake or strip
PLANS DATA
No. of sheets: 4
Level of detail: Above average
Cost per set: $60.00
WB Plan No. 94

See page 96 for further information.

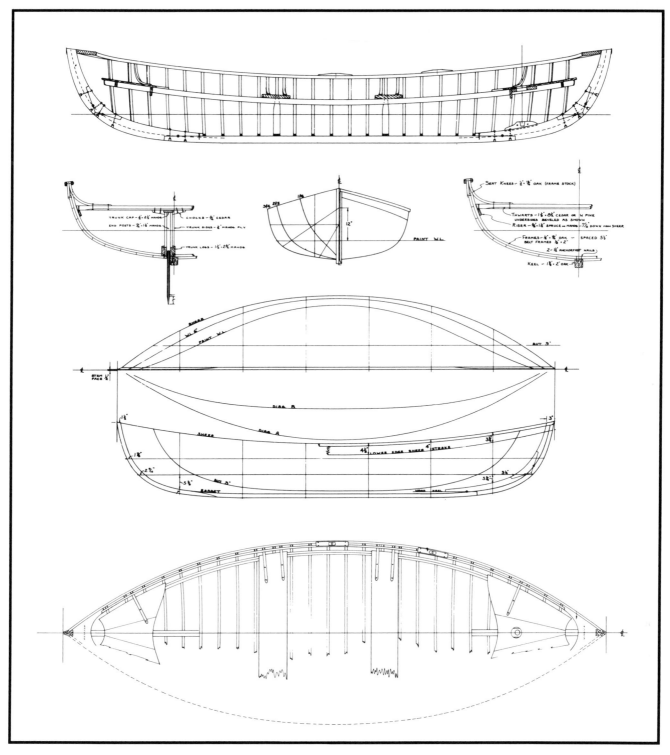

14'10" Outboard Skiff, Sprite

by Atkin & Co.

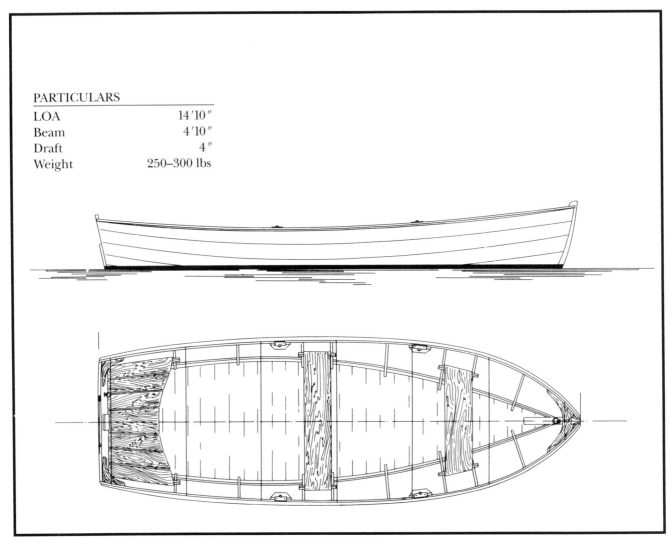

PARTICULARS

LOA	14'10"
Beam	4'10"
Draft	4"
Weight	250–300 lbs

Although the Atkins' fine drawings for Sprite show two rowing stations, this skiff makes no pretense of being a thoroughbred pulling boat. At 4'10" breadth (about 4'2" at the waterline) on 14'10" of length, she's simply too wide. Neither does her bottom show enough rocker, nor does it narrow down sufficiently at the stern to clear her run. And her substantial (for a rowing skiff) freeboard won't be welcome during a long pull to windward.

Of course, all of the characteristics that detract from her desirability as a pure pulling boat make Sprite nearly perfect as a knockabout outboard skiff. Her wide bottom and moderate rocker contribute to stability and the ability to carry weight (mechanical or human) back aft. You'll have no qualms about exiting over her transom or standing at full height to scrub down a big boat's topsides.

Sprite's high, flaring sides offer reserve buoyancy and stability—and they look fine. They're planked up with four lapped strakes of white cedar, and their shape will dis-courage any attempts at getting them out of sheet ply-wood. Of course, you could rip and scarf the sheets into appropriate planks and glue them together—but the advan-tages to such a scheme are unclear. Cedar is friendlier than plywood to tools and builders alike, and its aroma will give your boatshop all kinds of ambiance. Properly beveled and riveted, the laps will stay tight for longer than anyone is likely to care about. Be that as it may, if your skiff will live on a trailer or a beach, you might consider using sheet plywood for her bottom.

Building Sprite would make worthwhile use of, say, 60 to 80 hours of your time—next week, or 20 years down the road. Styles come and go, but there will always be room along the waterfront for a good flat-bottomed skiff.

Sprite's plans consist of how-to-build instructions and four large sheets of drawings: profile and plan views, hull lines, offsets, and construction plans. WB Plan No. 132, $60.00.

Plan 132

DESCRIPTION
Hull type: Flat-bottomed skiff
Construction: Cross-planked bottom, lapstrake sides

PERFORMANCE
*Suitable for: Protected waters
*Intended capacity: 1–4
Trailerable: Yes
Propulsion: Oars, 6-hp outboard

BUILDING DATA
Skill needed: Basic to intermediate
Lofting required: Yes
*Alternative construction: Plywood, glued-lapstrake
   plywood

PLANS DATA
No. of sheets: 4
Level of detail: Average
Cost per set: $60.00
WB Plan No. 132
*See page 96 for further information.

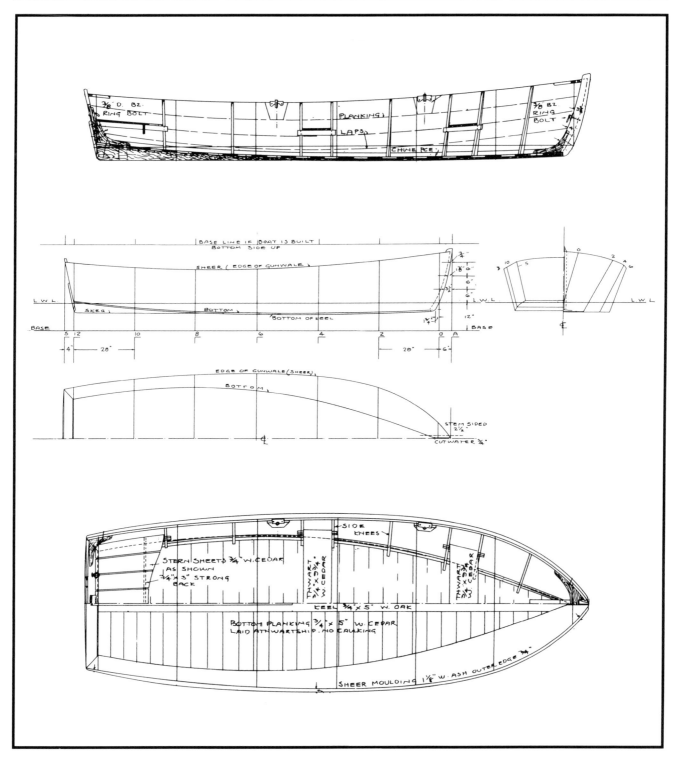

—25—

18' Pulling Boat, Liz

by Ken Bassett

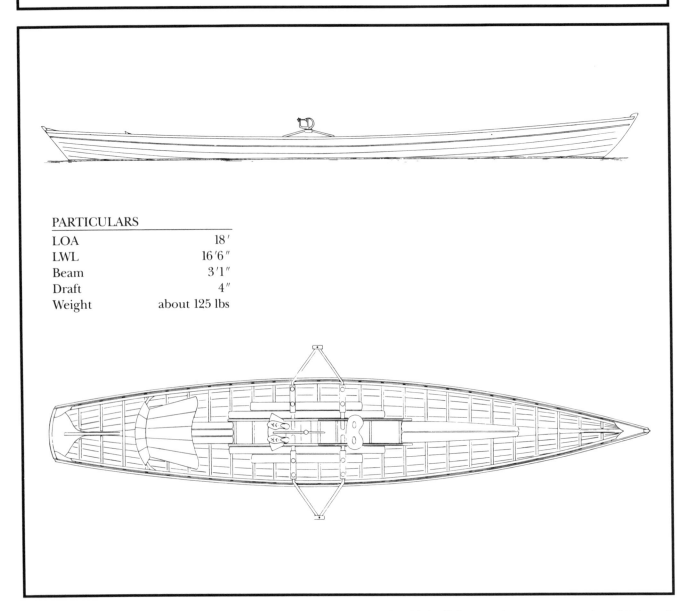

PARTICULARS

LOA	18'
LWL	16'6"
Beam	3'1"
Draft	4"
Weight	about 125 lbs

I'm sure it's happened to you, perhaps at a wooden boat show, a maritime museum, or maybe even one day on the waterfront. Suddenly before you is a small boat of such elegance of line, such exquisite proportion and workmanship, that it takes your breath away. How could anyone actually use this boat, you ask yourself? Such boats are almost invariably of traditional construction—modern methods usually just don't have the levels of intricate detail to pull off this kind of appearance.

In the hands of the right builder, Liz could be one of these boats. With all those steam-bent frames, copper rivets, and plank laps, she has lots to keep the eye busy. If her quarter knees and breasthook are shaped right and the optional curved transom carefully done, she'll melt the heart of even the most confirmed stitch-and-glue fanatic.

But Liz's sliding rowing seat shows that this boat is really intended to be used. With her 16'6" waterline and hull weight of only about 125 lbs, you'll really be able to cover some territory. Her buoyant ends and reasonable beam will ensure that a little rough water will not send you back to shore.

Of course, all this perfection comes at a price. Building Liz will not be a fast or easy job. It would be unrealistic to expect a perfect job from anything less than a well-experienced builder. On the other hand, even with a few mistakes, this would be a fun, rewarding boat to build and one that will be a pleasure to use.

The eight sheets of drawings include lines, construction, full-sized patterns for molds and transom, and plans for sliding seat and footrest. WB Plan No. 97, $90.00.

Plan 97

DESCRIPTION
Hull type: Round-bottomed, transom stern
Construction: Lapstrake planked over steamed frames

PERFORMANCE
*Suitable for: Protected waters
*Intended capacity: 1–2
Trailerable: Yes
Propulsion: Oars

BUILDING DATA
Skill needed: Advanced

Lofting required: No
*Alternative construction: Cold-molded, strip,
  glued lap

PLANS DATA
No. of sheets: 8
Level of detail: Above average
Cost per set: $90.00
WB Plan No. 97

See page 96 for further information.

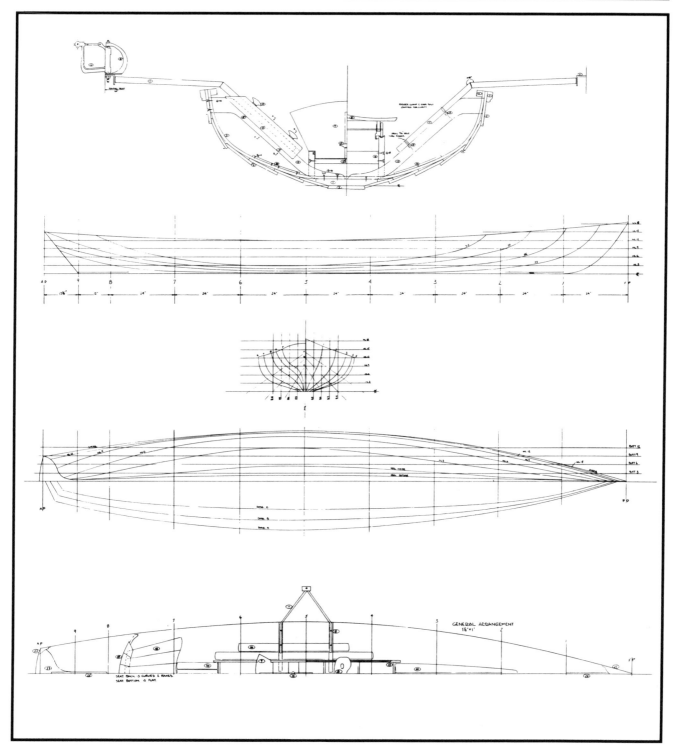

18' Pulling Boat, Firefly

by Ken Bassett

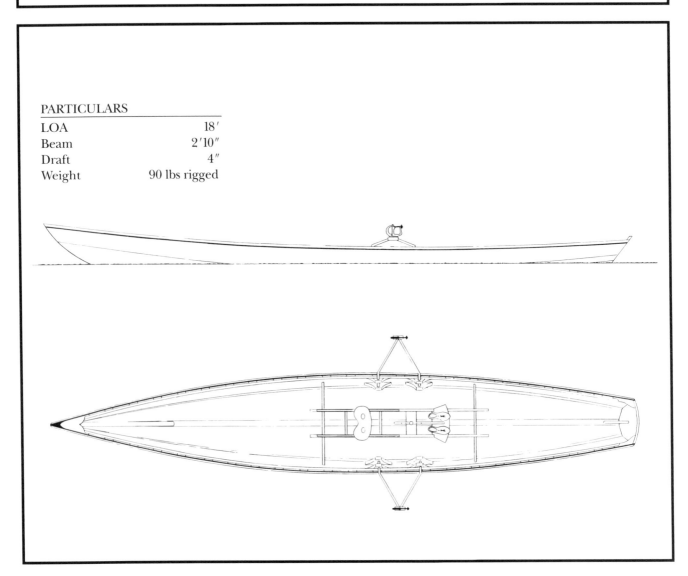

PARTICULARS

LOA	18'
Beam	2'10"
Draft	4"
Weight	90 lbs rigged

Rowing is good fun and good exercise, whether you're rowing a short, tubby little thing or a 28' sliding-seat machine. But most people will agree that going faster is more fun, and you can certainly see more of the scenery in a boat that will cover some territory. The key to going faster is a boat that is longer, lighter, and narrower. More horsepower is a big help, too, and that means bringing your legs, not just your back and arms, into the rowing action. This is where the sliding seat comes into the picture, and it brings with it a more all-around kind of exercise.

A high-performance rowing machine, however, can be a bit intimidating for the novice. The narrow beam means that stability is low, and these boats can be intolerant of mistakes. If you want to get started in performance rowing, or if you have enjoyed rowing a good fixed-seat boat but feel the urge to move up a notch, Firefly could be just the boat for you. Designed by Ken Bassett as an entry-level sliding-seat pulling boat, Firefly will provide healthful exercise and rewarding performance at a cruising speed of 20 strokes per minute. And with a beam of 34", there will be enough stability to keep a beginner out of trouble.

Construction calls for ¼" marine plywood over spruce keel and chines, with transom, gunwales, and sliding seat mechanism of native cherry, or other suitable hardwood, finished bright. The fledgling builder should not be afraid to tackle this boat, although a bit of woodworking experience will be helpful. Firefly's plans are well detailed, and even include drawings for the sliding-seat mechanism. No lofting is required, and materials are readily available.

Plans are printed on five sheets, including lines, construction, sliding seat and outrigger details, full-sized patterns for molds, transom, and stem, and hardware sources. WB Plan No. 121, $60.00.

Plan 121

DESCRIPTION
Hull type: V-bottomed, transom-sterned pulling boat
Construction: Plywood
PERFORMANCE
*Suitable for: Protected waters
*Intended capacity: 1
Trailerable: Cartoppable
Propulsion: Oars
BUILDING DATA
Skill needed: Basic to intermediate

Lofting required: No
*Alternative construction: None
PLANS DATA
No. of sheets: 5
Level of detail: Above average
Cost per set: $60.00
WB Plan No. 121

*See page 96 for further information.

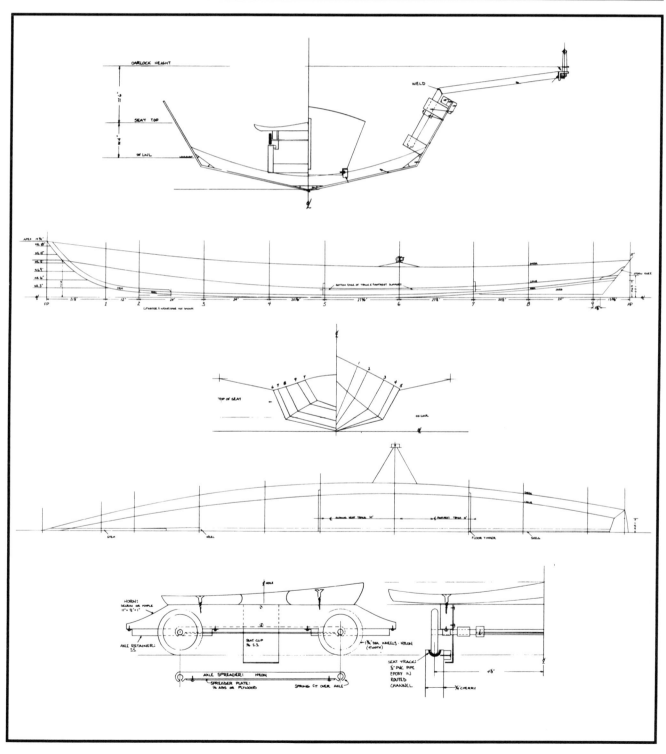

27' Recreational Double Shell, Kookaburra

by Graeme King

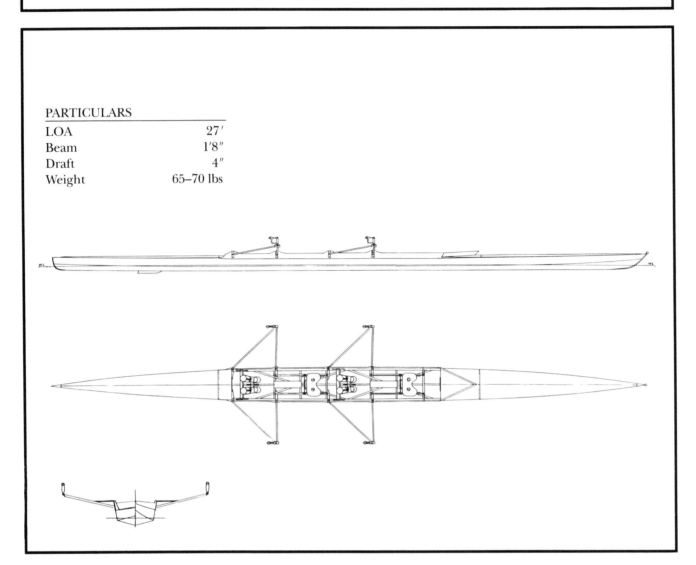

PARTICULARS

LOA	27'
Beam	1'8"
Draft	4"
Weight	65–70 lbs

Graeme King is one of the world's top builders of wooden racing shells. His 22'6" Kingfisher recreational single shell (designed in 1983 at the request of WoodenBoat magazine) has proven to be virtually unbeatable when it comes to rowing fast in rough water. And its rakish V-bottomed hull sets this striking boat apart from the fleet of round-bottomed competitors.

Now, King has stretched the Kingfisher to 27' in length—making room for another oarsman and making an already very fast boat even faster. But the new double will be no more difficult to build than the old single.

Named Kookaburra, in honor of the largest (and possibly loudest) bird in the Kingfisher family, this fine double is built with ³⁄₃₂" or ⅛" sheets of mahogany plywood and weighs in at only 65–70 lbs. We hesitate to describe any rowing shell as stable, but this boat (with its hard chines and 1'8" beam at the rails) is far easier to balance than the narrower, circular-sectioned competition boats. Yet Kookaburra retains some 93% of the racing boats' speed.

In competitive rowing, the light weight and responsiveness of the double scull (two crew members, each pulling two oars) make it a favorite with experienced oarsmen. Kookaburra is technically a double scull, but that nicety of terminology seems to have been lost in the recreational fleet. Whatever we might call it, Kookaburra will combine much of the speed and spirit of the racing boats with greater stability and a more secure ride in a chop.

Kookaburra is a boat in which you and your partner can spend hours lazily exploring local estuaries. Or, when so inclined, you can sprint down the bay at more than 10 mph while getting some of the most rigorous (yet gentle on your joints) whole-body exercise available.

Kookaburra's well-detailed plans are on four sheets and include: general arrangement, fittings details, bulkhead details, and drawings for the strongback. WB Plan No. 135, $90.00.

Plan 135

DESCRIPTION
Hull type: V-bottomed shell
Construction: Plywood planking over bulkhead-type
  frames
PERFORMANCE
*Suitable for: Protected waters
*Intended capacity: 2
  Cartoppable
  Propulsion: Oars
BUILDING DATA
Skill needed: Intermediate

Lofting required: No
*Alternative construction: None
  Helpful information: "Building the Kingfisher,"
  Parts I, II, and III by Graeme King. WB Nos. 61,
  62, and 63 or monograph.
PLANS DATA
No. of sheets: 4
Level of detail: Above average
Cost per set: $90.00
WB Plan No. 135

See page 96 for further information.

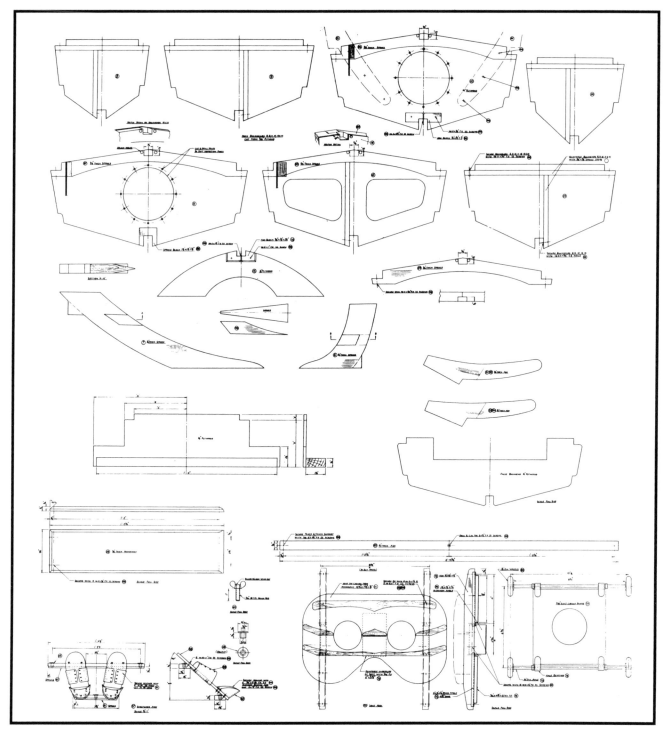

13'4" and 16' Melonseed Skiffs

by Marc Barto

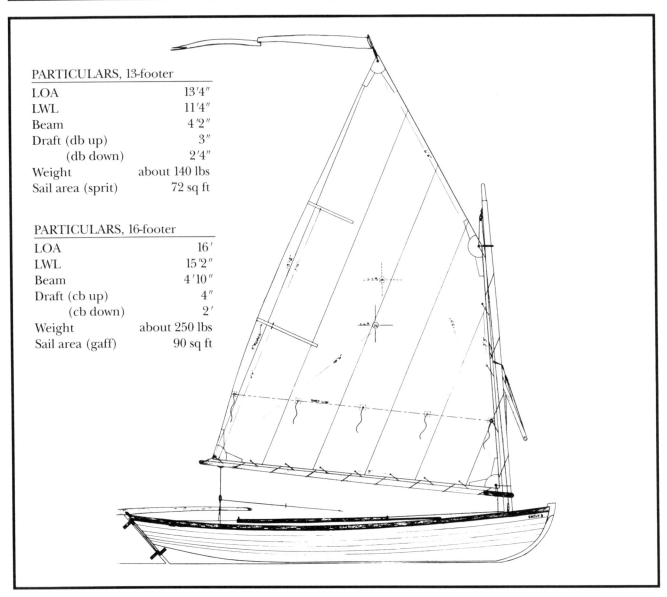

PARTICULARS, 13-footer

LOA	13'4"
LWL	11'4"
Beam	4'2"
Draft (db up)	3"
(db down)	2'4"
Weight	about 140 lbs
Sail area (sprit)	72 sq ft

PARTICULARS, 16-footer

LOA	16'
LWL	15'2"
Beam	4'10"
Draft (cb up)	4"
(cb down)	2'
Weight	about 250 lbs
Sail area (gaff)	90 sq ft

The marshes and paper-thin reaches of New Jersey's Barnegat Bay demand boats that can sail—really sail, not simply float—in water less than one foot deep. The famous Barnegat Bay sneakboxes, low on freeboard and blunt of shape, evolved to meet the needs of 19th-century duck hunters (market gunners) who supplied the tables of nearby Philadelphia and New York City.

The melonseed is a lesser-known (and now extinct) duck gunning skiff from the Jersey shore. More able (and, we think, more handsome) than the sneakboxes, these round-bilged skiffs hunted the open reaches of the coastal lagoons beyond the protection of the salt marshes.

Designer Marc Barto's new lapstrake-plywood Melonseed Skiffs make great daysailers—whether or not you intend to blast ducks out of the sky. With their shapely wineglass transoms and substantial flare, these hulls are easily driven and dry in a chop. Although the cockpits are not overly large, they are well proportioned and relatively clear of intrusion. The well-crowned decks offer plenty of comfortable sprawling space.

The gaff and sprit rigs provide more than enough power to drive these surprisingly stable hulls at good speed. And the short spars are easily made and stowed. Shallow barn-door rudders and wide, flat keels make for easy trailering.

The Melonseeds' plans consist of 10 sheets that show, among other details: the lines, construction plan, offsets, sail plan, strongback, molds, and planking details. WB Plan No. 119 (13'4" hull) and WB Plan No. 120 (16' hull), $90.00 each.

Plans 119 and 120

DESCRIPTION
Hull type: Round-bottomed daysailer
Rig: Sprit (13-footer); gaff (16-footer)
Construction: Lapstrake-plywood planking over
  steam-bent frames
PERFORMANCE
*Suitable for: Protected waters
*Intended capacity: 1–2 (13-footer), 1–4 (16-footer)
Trailerable: Yes
Propulsion: Sail

BUILDING DATA
Skill needed: Intermediate
Lofting required: No
*Alternative construction: Cold-molded, strip
PLANS DATA
No. of sheets: 10
Level of detail: Above average
Cost per set: $90.00 each
WB Plan No. 119 (13-footer) and No. 120 (16-footer)

See page 96 for further information.

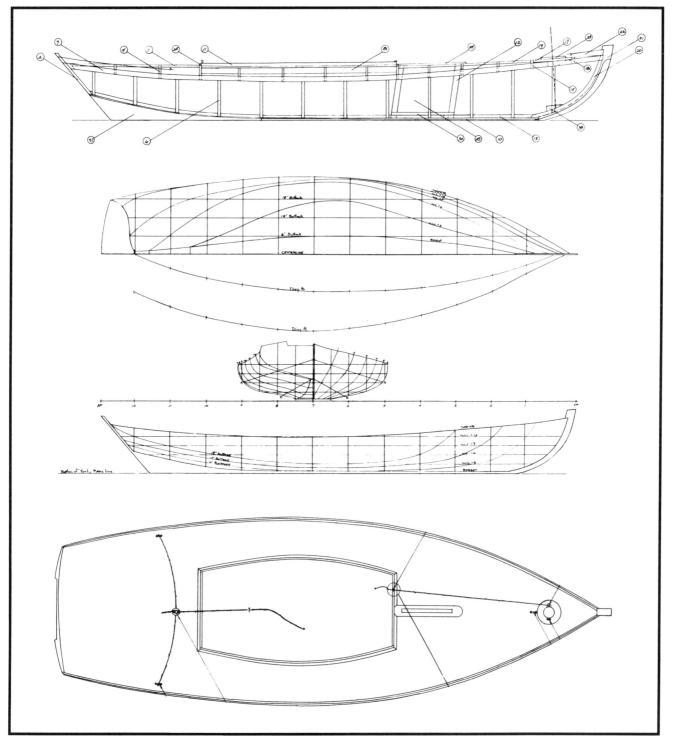

14'6" Whilly Boat

by Iain Oughtred

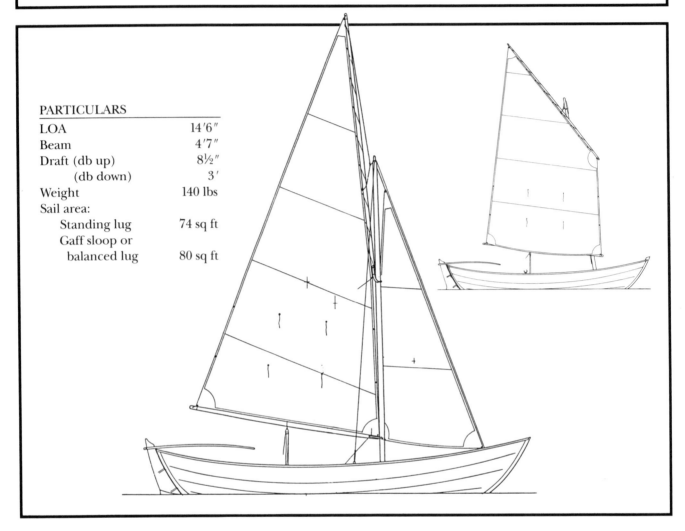

PARTICULARS

LOA	14'6"
Beam	4'7"
Draft (db up)	8½"
(db down)	3'
Weight	140 lbs
Sail area:	
Standing lug	74 sq ft
Gaff sloop or	
balanced lug	80 sq ft

Iain Oughtred based this appealing little double-ender on the Shetland ness yoles and sixerns. These workboats, in turn, can trace their heritage back to Norwegian roots— a fine origin for any small boat.

The hull lines for this 14'6" daysailer and beach cruiser possess a timeless universality. Sailors who have grown up in the surf will recognize the balanced ends, strong sheer, ample reserve buoyancy, and the light-but-strong construction as desirable traits in any small boat that must handle breakers and beaches.

The Whilly Boat's construction makes good use of plywood and epoxy. Four wide strakes for each side are spiled, hung over temporary molds, and beveled. Drywall screws can act as clamps until the epoxy sets. Solid lumber should not be used for planking this hull—lack of cross-grain strength makes it prone to splitting, especially along the laps.

As is his practice, Oughtred offers the Whilly Boat's builders several options. He describes three different sailing rigs: an 80-sq-ft gaff sloop; a 74-sq-ft boomless standing lug; and an 80-sq-ft balanced lug.

You have a choice of building a pivoting centerboard and kick-up rudder (desirable if you're going to sail in thin water) or, for use in deeper water, a daggerboard and fixed rudder blade.

Oughtred shows optional forward and after decks; both are drawn below the rails. This arrangement looks fine as it allows our eyes to follow the sheer uninterrupted from stem to sternpost, and it gives better access to the ends of the boat.

The Whilly Boat offers the independence desired by all solo sailors. She's as able as an open boat of her size can be. She'll sail you just about anywhere within reason, and you can row her home if the wind dies. You'll not need mechanical assistance (although Oughtred shows an optional motorwell), or a boatyard, or a chandlery. And when you think of her shape, you'll smile.

The plans for the Whilly Boat include a 15-page instruction booklet and five large sheets of drawings: hull lines, construction plan, sail plans, full-sized stem patterns, and full-sized mold patterns. WB Plan No. 104, $90.00.

Plan 104

DESCRIPTION
Hull type: Multi-chine/lapstrake, double-ender
Rig: Standing lug or gaff sloop
Construction: Glued-lapstrake plywood

PERFORMANCE
*Suitable for: Protected waters
*Intended capacity: 1–4
Trailerable: Yes
Propulsion: Sail, oars, outboard

BUILDING DATA
Skill needed: Intermediate
Lofting required: No
*Alternative construction: None

PLANS DATA
No. of sheets: 5 plus instruction booklet
Level of detail: Above average
Cost per set: $90.00
WB Plan No. 104
*See page 96 for further information.

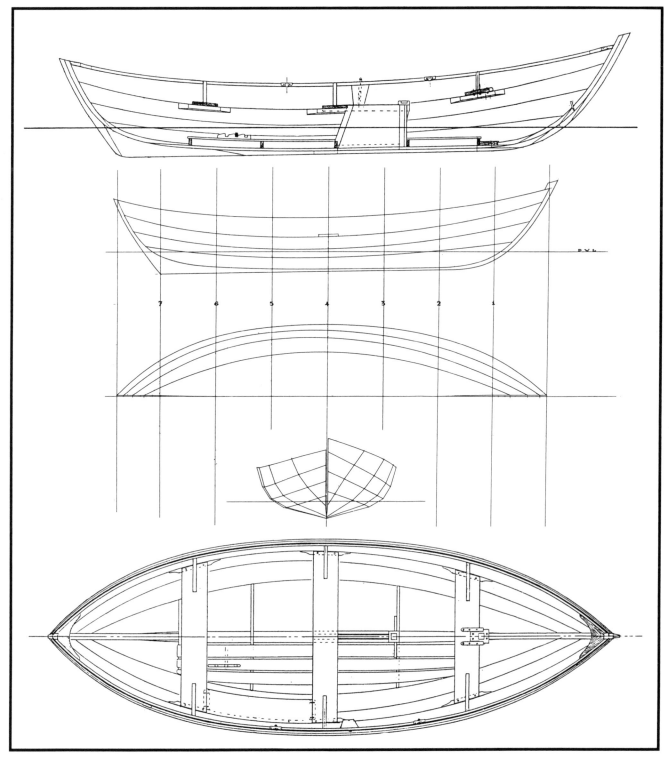

15' Catboat, Marsh Cat

by Joel White

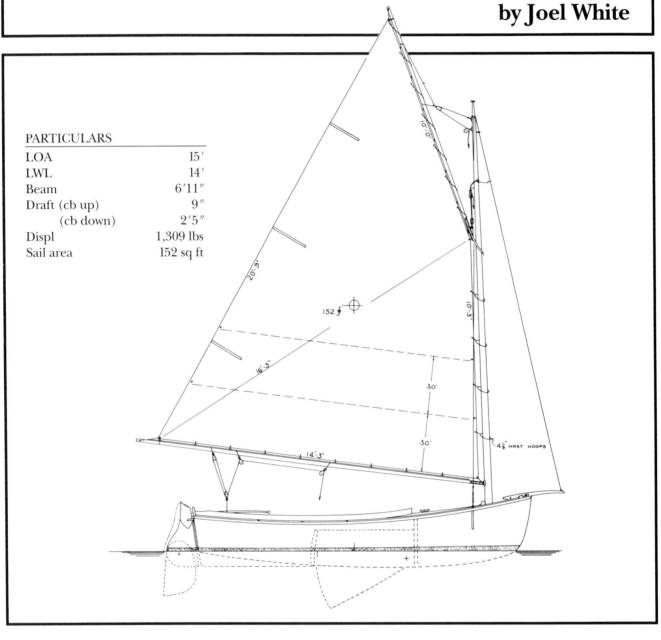

PARTICULARS

LOA	15'
LWL	14'
Beam	6'11"
Draft (cb up)	9"
(cb down)	2'5"
Displ	1,309 lbs
Sail area	152 sq ft

Catboat owners tend to be a pretty devoted bunch and will seldom countenance any disparaging remarks on the type. There are some good reasons for their affection. Foot for foot, it would be hard to find a bigger boat than a catboat. The great beam that provides all that room makes a catboat sail on her feet—having lunch while sailing is not such a scramble. For those who enjoy relaxed sailing rather than fiddling with lines, a catboat's single, self-tending sail will be just the thing. And then there are submerged rocks and ledges to be avoided and, here too, the catboat excels, for with such shallow draft you can usually see an underwater obstruction before there is any threat.

Joel White's long experience with small catboats shows in the Marsh Cat's lines. With slightly less beam and a bit more bow overhang than many of her type, she will dis-

play good manners to go along with her good looks. Her cold-molded construction results in a light, tight hull that is well suited to trailering.

White's six sheets of plans leave little guesswork for the beginner, and they include many touches that would make an old salt nod with approval. Since there are no reverse curves in her hull sections, planking veneers should go on without a fuss. This will not be a quick boat to build, but she'll be long lasting and relatively low in maintenance requirements.

The six-sheet set of plans includes: lines, full-sized patterns (for molds, stem, and expanded transom—no lofting needed), construction, sail and spar plans, lumber and fastening list, full-sized hardware drawings, and even directions for making ballast bags. WB Plan No. 95, $90.00.

Plan 95

DESCRIPTION
Hull type: Round-bottomed, centerboard boat
Rig: Gaff cat
Construction: Cold-molded

PERFORMANCE
*Suitable for: Protected waters
*Intended capacity: 1–5 daysailing
Trailerable: Yes
Propulsion: Sail, oars, outboard

BUILDING DATA
Skill needed: Intermediate
Lofting required: No
*Alternative construction: Carvel, lapstrake, strip

PLANS DATA
No. of sheets: 6
Level of detail: Above average
Cost per set: $90.00
WB Plan No. 95

*See page 96 for further information.

—37—

16' Perfect Skiff

by Stephen Weld

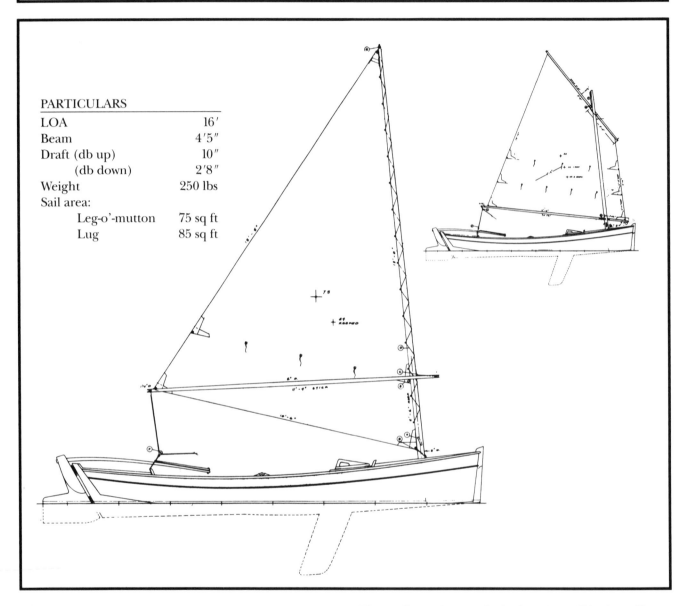

PARTICULARS

LOA	16'
Beam	4'5"
Draft (db up)	10"
(db down)	2'8"
Weight	250 lbs
Sail area:	
Leg-o'-mutton	75 sq ft
Lug	85 sq ft

As a type, the flat-bottomed skiff can be both the most and the least refined craft afloat. Popular for their ease of construction (any handy fisherman, working by eye, can knock one together in a day or two), they provide a rugged utility craft. But as easy as they are to build, good skiffs can be devilishly hard to design. Everything must be just right to get the best from this type of hull. As the winner of WoodenBoat's 1991 Skiff Design Competition, Stephen Weld has sought to combine the best work of many students of the flat-bottomed skiff—Culler, Chapelle, Bolger, and Redmond—into what is indeed a tall order: the Perfect Skiff.

Two construction methods are provided for this boat. The modern plywood-and-epoxy version will be lighter, more suitable for trailering, and require less maintenance.

The traditional cross-planked version will be friendlier to build, less skittish when boarding, and will, in time, take on a graceful patina that is outside the realm of plywood. Two rigs are shown as well. The leg-o'-mutton rig has simplicity and performance going for it, but the lugsail can be doused more easily if conditions dust up, and its shorter spars will stow completely inside the boat.

The Perfect Skiff would be a good first project for the beginning boatbuilder. She will provide the easiest lofting lesson possible, and her construction is exhaustively detailed in the two-part article "Building the Perfect Skiff" (WB Nos. 111 and 112).

Plans are printed on five sheets, and include lines, construction for plywood and cedar-planked versions, lug and leg-o'-mutton sail plans. WB Plan No. 106, $75.00.

Plan 106

DESCRIPTION
Hull type: Flat-bottomed skiff
Rig: Leg-o'-mutton or balanced lug
Construction: Plywood planking over bulkhead frames
PERFORMANCE
*Suitable for: Protected waters
*Intended capacity: 1–4
Trailerable: Yes
Propulsion: Sail, oars
BUILDING DATA
Skill needed: Basic to intermediate

Lofting required: Yes
Alternative construction: Cross-planked bottom,
  planked sides (details included)
"How to Build" instructions: WB Nos. 110–112
PLANS DATA
No. of sheets: 5
Level of detail: Average
Cost per set: $75.00
WB Plan No. 106

See page 96 for further information.

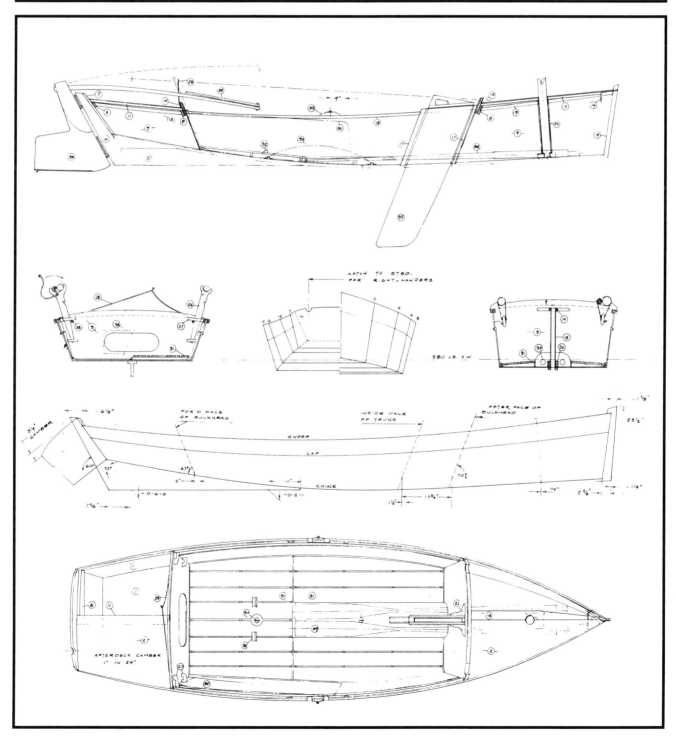

—39—

16' Quattro Catamaran

by Richard and Lilian Woods

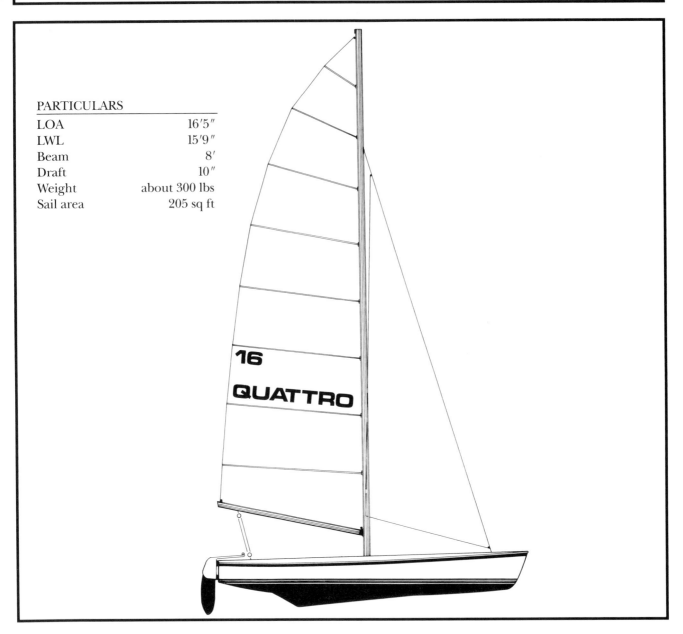

PARTICULARS

LOA	16'5"
LWL	15'9"
Beam	8'
Draft	10"
Weight	about 300 lbs
Sail area	205 sq ft

Building plans for really good high-performance beach cats are hard to find. Here's a great one. Designed by the successful British team of Richard and Lilian Woods, the Quattro 16 is striking to look at and exciting to sail.

Lighter than most similar production boats, the Quattro can be carried up the beach by a couple. Early reports from England indicate that this easily built plywood multihull sails faster than the ubiquitous Hobie 16 on all points.

The Woods' unusually well detailed plans will guide you step-by-step through the construction of the simple and rugged stitch-and-glue plywood hulls. The crossbeams consist of aluminum mast extrusions, strong and easily

obtained. The forward beam (missing from some production cats of similar size) keeps the hulls from being pulled cross-eyed by tension in the bridle. This allows a higher-aspect-ratio jib to be set lower on the boat—most efficient.

The delta-shaped skeg-keels provide lateral resistance and sharp control without the complications of centerboard trunks.

Quattro's plans consist of two large sheets of drawings and a fully illustrated instruction booklet, including: sail plan, patterns (no lofting needed), construction details and hints, and a list of necessary materials. WB Plan No. 125, $90.00.

Plan 125

DESCRIPTION
Hull type: V-bottomed catamaran
Rig: Sloop
Construction: Stitch-and-glue plywood over
  bulkhead frames

PERFORMANCE
*Suitable for: Protected waters
*Intended capacity: 1–2
  Trailerable: Yes
  Propulsion: Sail

BUILDING DATA
Skill needed: Basic
Lofting required: No
*Alternative construction: None

PLANS DATA
No. of sheets: 2 sheets and building booklet
Level of detail: Above average
Cost per set: $90.00
WB Plan No. 125

See page 96 for further information.

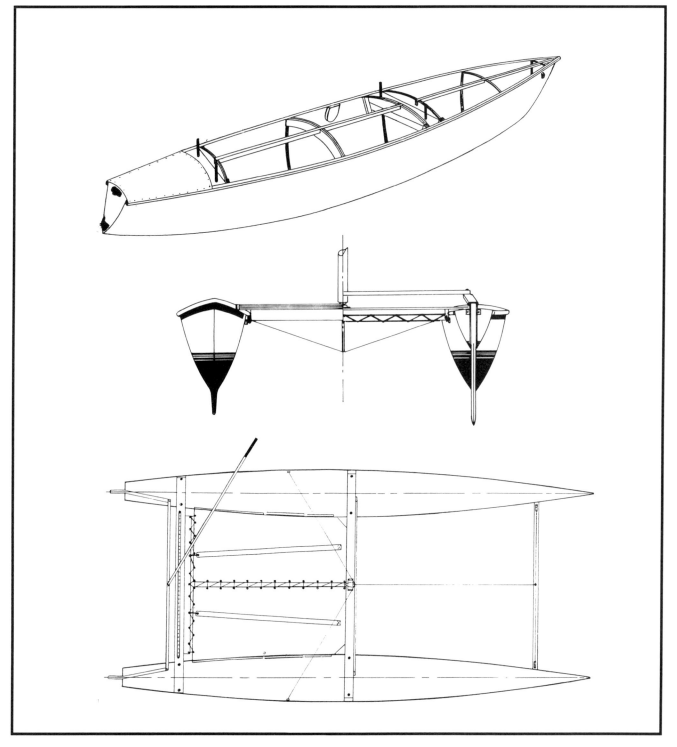

19'6" Caledonia Yawl

by Iain Oughtred

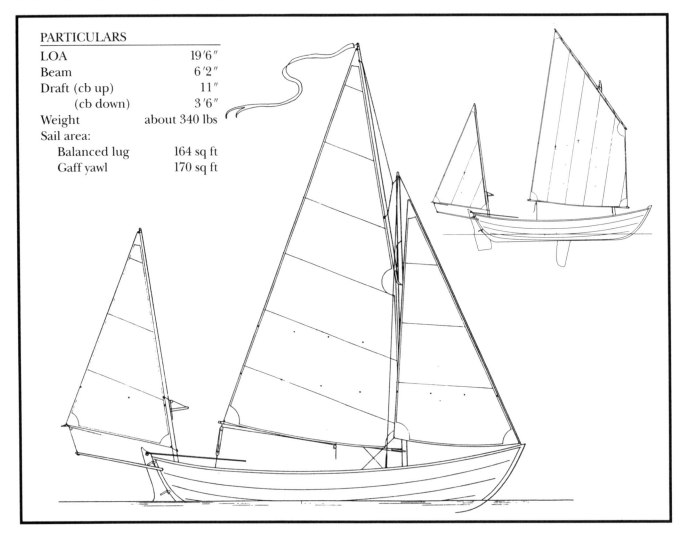

PARTICULARS	
LOA	19'6"
Beam	6'2"
Draft (cb up)	11"
(cb down)	3'6"
Weight	about 340 lbs
Sail area:	
Balanced lug	164 sq ft
Gaff yawl	170 sq ft

Designer Iain Oughtred is known for applying an artist's touch to his light lapstrake creations. He admits to having been under the influence of Shetland ness yoles and sixerns while drawing this handsome double-ender.

The Caledonia has relatively high ends and shows considerable reserve buoyancy above the waterline throughout its length. The hull lines resemble those of many surfboats that have evolved to meet the rigors of working off exposed beaches. Oughtred gave her a run that is finer and shows more deadrise than might be ideal for extremely high speed under sail, but the resulting gains in helm balance and civilized behavior in waves make the compromise worthwhile.

Caledonia's builders can rig their boats with either balanced lug or high-peaked gaff-headed mainsails. The balanced lug has the advantage of being self-vanging and simple. It sets on an unstayed mast, and it requires less time for raising and striking than does the gaff rig.

Caledonia's lapstrake and epoxy hull is built in an inverted position. The backbone and building jig are fairly conventional. Drywall screws clamp the plywood strakes together until the epoxy sets. (Lack of cross-grain strength makes solid timber unsuitable for planking this boat.)

As for accommodations, Oughtred shows a version with considerable built-in closed space (similar to a Drascombe Lugger's interior) and a more open model. The open boat will be simpler and lighter, but builders can choose various combinations of the two layouts. In all cases, the decks are kept below the rails. This arrangement gives better access to the yawl's ends, and it permits secure on-deck stowage of light gear. Also, the sunken decks allow your eyes to follow the full, unbroken sweep of the sheer from stem to stern—and a lovely sheer it is.

Plans for the Caledonia Yawl consist of eight sheets: hull lines, construction, mold patterns, stem and stern-post patterns, and sail plans. Also included are three sheets of specifications and 13 pages of lapstrake-plywood building instructions. WB Plan No. 103, $150.00.

Plan 103

DESCRIPTION
Hull type: Multi-chine/lapstrake, double-ended
   centerboard boat
Rig: Yawl, with lug or gaff mainsail
Construction: Glued lapstrake plywood

PERFORMANCE
*Suitable for: Protected waters
*Intended capacity: 1–6
 Trailerable: Yes
 Propulsion: Sail, oars

BUILDING DATA
Skill needed: Intermediate to advanced
Lofting required: No
*Alternative construction: None

PLANS DATA
No. of sheets: 8 plus instruction booklet
Level of detail: Above average
Cost per set: $150.00
WB Plan No. 103

See page 96 for further information.

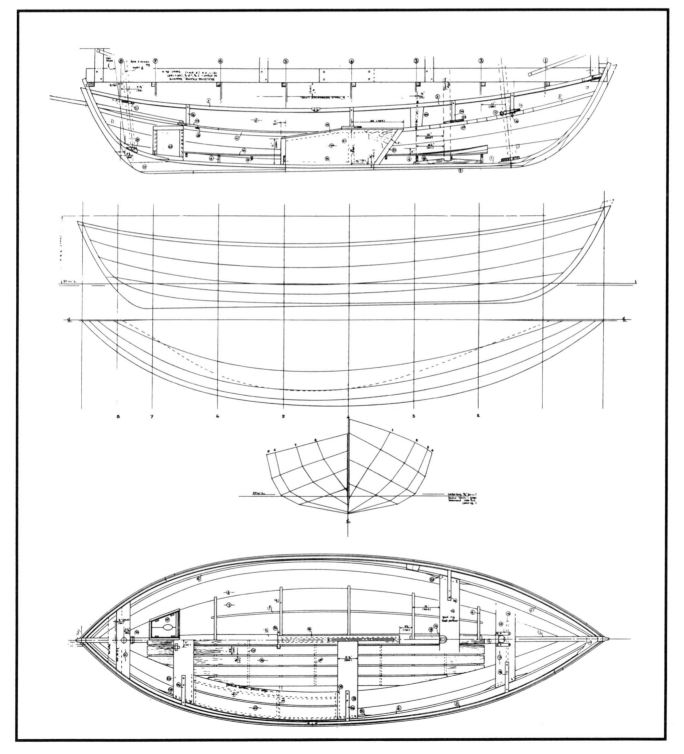

—43—

20'3" Flatfish Class Sloop

by Joel White

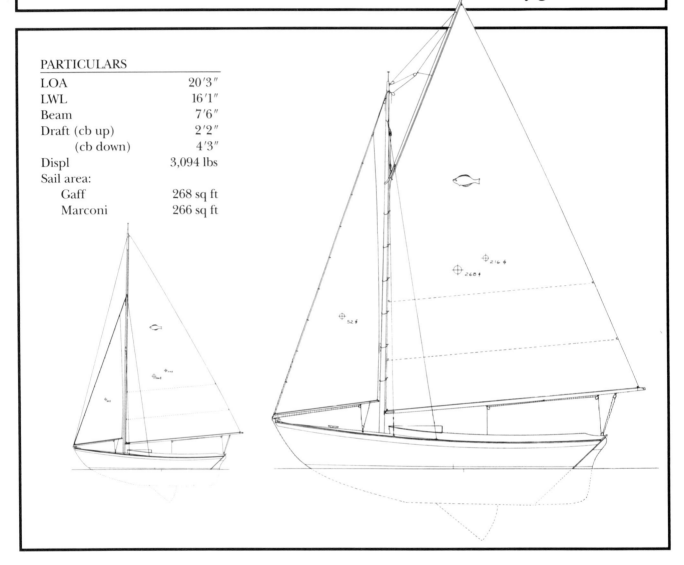

PARTICULARS

LOA	20'3"
LWL	16'1"
Beam	7'6"
Draft (cb up)	2'2"
(cb down)	4'3"
Displ	3,094 lbs
Sail area:	
Gaff	268 sq ft
Marconi	266 sq ft

The winter of 1913 saw the great Nathanael G. Herreshoff wintering in Bermuda, with a new boat, ALERION, designed for his own use. He was so pleased with this new design that most of his subsequent small sailboat designs could trace their lineage to her. In 1914 came the wonderful 12½-footer, and the next winter brought a somewhat larger version, known as the Fish class. The boats in Alerion's extended family, including the Buzzard's Bay 25s, the Newport 29s, and the Fishers Island 31s, share certain traits—shapely hulls, fast sailing, impeccable manners, and long lives.

In 1986, WoodenBoat introduced the Haven 12½-footer, designer Joel White's centerboard version of the Herreshoff 12½. These boats were so successful and the design so well received that Joel was persuaded to design a similar centerboard conversion of the Fish class boat which he has named Flatfish.

Like the Haven 12½, the Flatfish will require an accom-

plished builder. With the exception of the centerboard and its case, the original scantlings and construction details are used throughout, and Herreshoff drew his designs with the skilled builders of his day in mind. In addition, this hull must be carefully lofted if the full beauty of Flatfish's hull is to be realized. WoodenBoat's monograph *How to Build the Haven 12½-Footer* will provide valuable help to the Flatfish builder as well, as the two boats are very similar in construction.

The result will be more than worth the effort, as this boat must surely be one of the most lovely and able daysailers ever conceived. Yes, a well-built Flatfish, with proper care, will be a cherished possession for generations to come.

Plans are printed on six sheets, and include lines and offsets, construction, gaff and marconi sail plans, and details for spars, hardware, and ballast keel. WB Plan No. 129, $150.00.

Plan 129

DESCRIPTION
Hull type: Round-bottomed, keel/centerboard
Rig: Gaff or marconi sloop
Construction: Carvel planked over steam-bent frames
PERFORMANCE
*Suitable for: Somewhat protected waters
*Intended capacity: 1–5 daysailing
Trailerable: Yes
Propulsion: Sail
BUILDING DATA
Skill needed: Advanced

Lofting required: Yes
*Alternative construction: None
Helpful information: *How to Build the Haven 12 ½-Footer*, by Maynard Bray
PLANS DATA
No. of sheets: 6
Level of detail: Average
Cost per set: $150.00
WB Plan No. 129

See page 96 for further information.

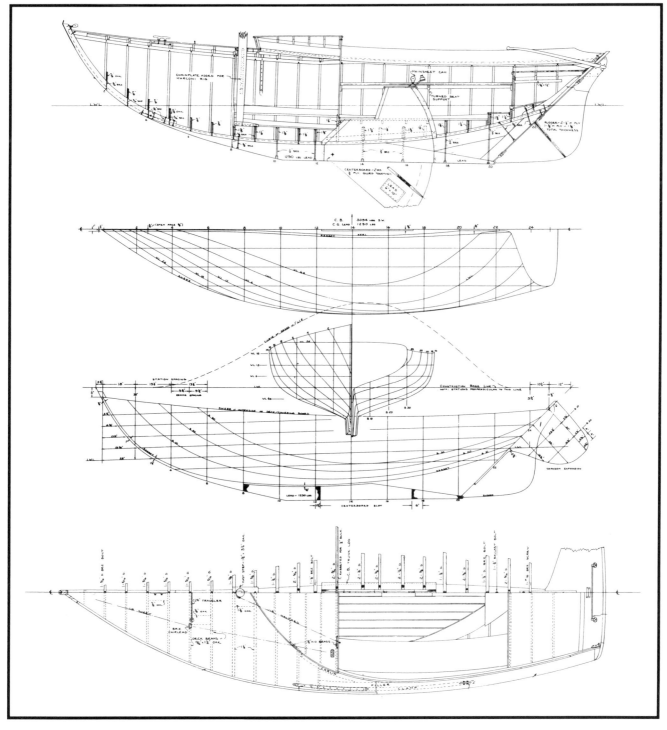

22′ Fox Island Class Sloop

by Joel White

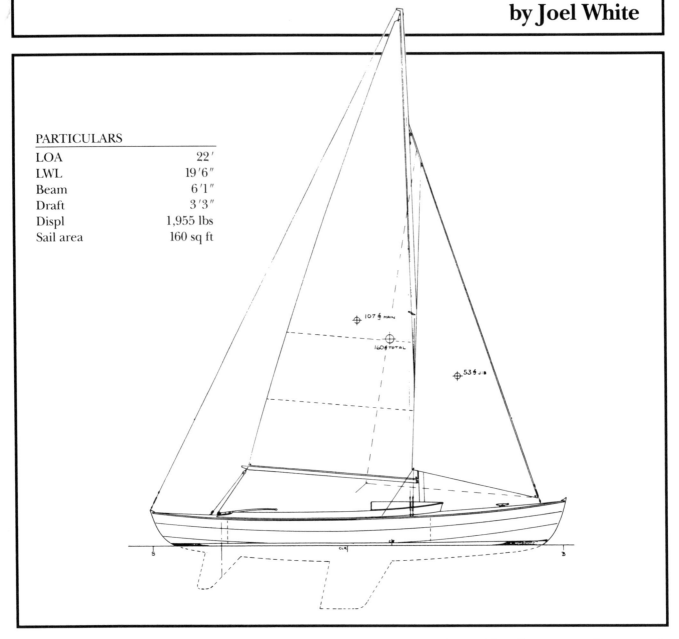

PARTICULARS

LOA	22′
LWL	19′6″
Beam	6′1″
Draft	3′3″
Displ	1,955 lbs
Sail area	160 sq ft

Seldom will you find a boat that combines genuine traditional good looks and modern performance. Perhaps few designers today know what traditional boats really look like, or how boats were detailed in the days when even shop tools and machinery were designed to please the eye. Joel White's long experience caring for classic yachts shows in the lovely sheer and fine detailing of the Fox Island class sloop.

White's love of fast sailing shows as well. Double-ended boats that are fast under sail can be difficult to draw, but a look at the modern fin keel and flat buttock lines lets you know that this is a boat intended for speed. You can be pretty sure that not many sailboats in her size range will pass her. While designed primarily for spirited daysailing and class racing, equipped with a boom tent and a sporting crew she could easily accommodate a couple for a weekend.

Although not specifically drawn for the beginning builder, the Fox Island class would not be a difficult boat to build. Lofting is required, but the hull is an easy one to loft, and the glued-lapstrake plywood construction method is one of the best for amateur builders. The fin keel, perhaps the most difficult part of this boat, can be cast to order (the plans list several foundries capable of the job). If you're short of time or unsure of your skills, Skiff Craft of Ohio, a long-time builder of lapstrake boats, offers Fox Island boats at any state of completion, from pre-cut parts to completed hulls. Plans are on four well-detailed sheets: lines, construction, keel and rudder details, and sail plan. WB Plan No. 101, $100.00.

Plan 101

DESCRIPTION
Hull type: Multi-chine/lapstrake, outside-ballasted
  keel boat
Rig: Sloop
Construction: Glued-lapstrake plywood over
  laminated frames
Featured in WB No. 112
PERFORMANCE
*Suitable for: Somewhat protected waters
*Intended capacity: 1–5 daysailing
  Trailerable: With difficulty

Propulsion: Sail
BUILDING DATA
Skill needed: Intermediate
Lofting required: Yes
*Alternative construction: None
PLANS DATA
No. of sheets: 4
Level of detail: Average
Cost per set: $100.00
WB Plan No. 101

See page 96 for further information.

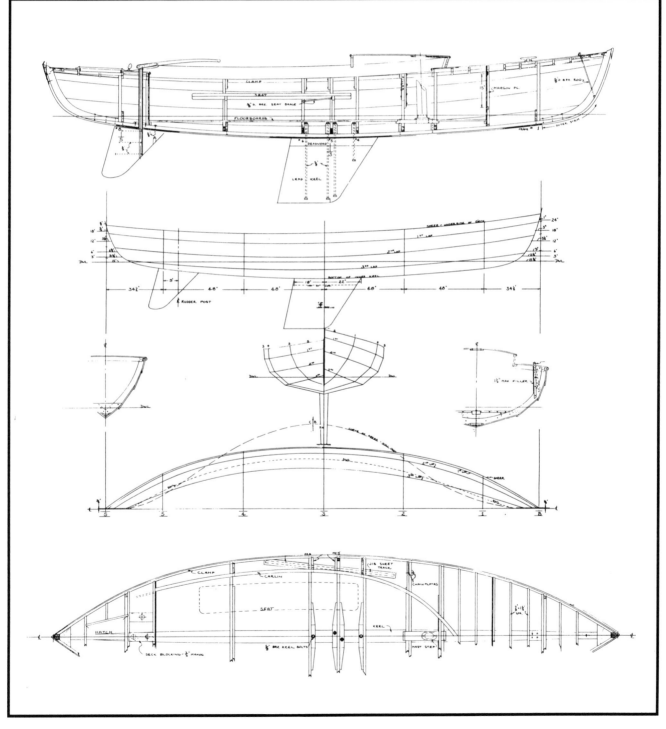

—47—

23' Centerboard Sloop

by Joel White

PARTICULARS

LOA	23'
LWL	18'8"
Beam	6'1"
Draft (cb up)	1'10"
(cb down)	5'9"
Displ	2,000 lbs
Sail area	193 sq ft

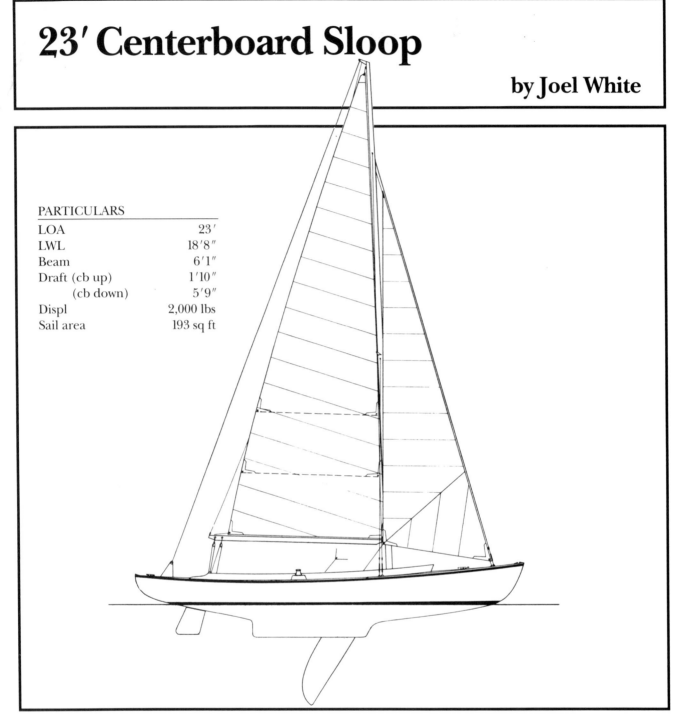

A fast daysailer can be a designer's dream come true. Compared to most other types of craft, such a boat need have few compromises—no worries about headroom, accommodations, or rating rules. Speed, good looks, and comfortable seating were Joel White's main criteria for this boat, and these requirements are not at all contradictory.

Similar in concept to White's Fox Island class, this boat could perhaps be considered a "no holds barred" version of that plywood lapstrake hull. For mathematically oriented sailors, this boat has some impressive numbers—displacement/length ratio of 136, sail area/displacement ratio of 19.4, ballast/displacement ratio of 52%. Those of you who don't care about numbers can just revel in her elegant lines and the promise of some very fast and spirited sailing.

Of course, this emphasis on performance has its cost. This will not be an easy boat to build; considerable lofting experience is required, and that lovely rounded stern could be a trial to plank. (A transom-sterned version is included that will be easier to build and perhaps even faster under sail.) The bulbed ballast keel will require some advanced casting skills. But offsetting these difficulties is one of the most complete sets of plans you are ever likely to see. Detailed drawings cover the ballast keel, metalwork, centerboard, and rudder.

Plans are printed on thirteen sheets and include lines for both double-ended and transom versions, construction, bulkhead and backbone details, and much more. WB Plan No. 128, $150.00.

Plan 128

DESCRIPTION

Hull type: Round-bottomed, keel/centerboard daysailer

Rig: Sloop

Construction: Cold-molded over strip-planked inner skin

Featured in WB Nos. 105, 126

PERFORMANCE

*Suitable for: Somewhat protected waters

*Intended capacity: 1–5 daysailing

Trailerable: Yes

Propulsion: Sail

BUILDING DATA

Skill needed: Advanced

Lofting required: Yes

*Alternative construction: Strip, carvel planked (transom stern)

PLANS DATA

No. of sheets: 13

Level of detail: Above average

Cost per set: $150.00

WB Plan No. 128

See page 96 for further information.

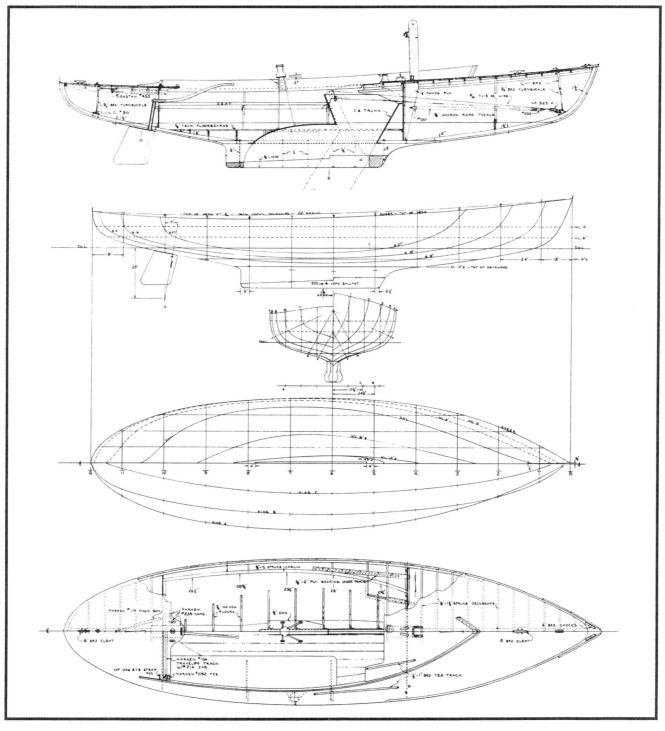

14'10" Runabout, Rascal

by Ken Bassett

PARTICULARS

LOA	14'10"
Beam	5'4"
Draft	6"
Weight (equipped)	about 790 lbs

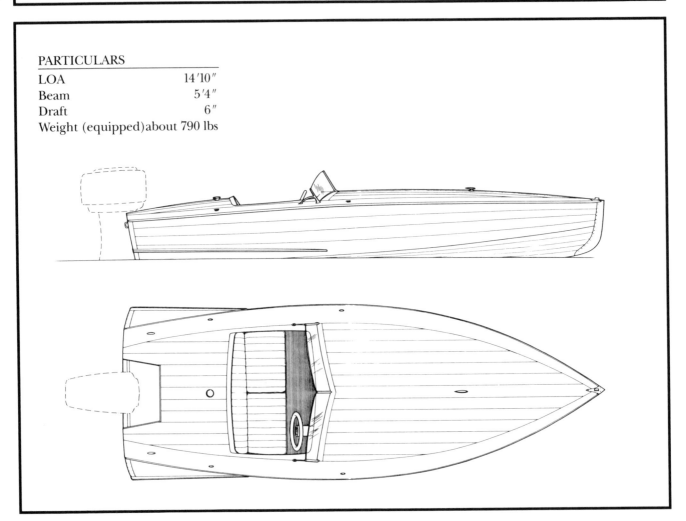

Rascal, a waterborne "roadster," reflects the functional philosophy of sports car design: maximum performance, and fun, for a given engine power.

Designer Ken Bassett set out to combine the look and feel of classic runabouts with the economy and practicality of outboard motors, highway trailers, plywood, and epoxy. He recommends this boat to anyone who would rather drive a Porsche than a Volkswagen.

Rascal goes together with an inner layer of plywood (4mm for the sides and 5mm for the bottom) ripped into 1'-wide planks and laid diagonally over transverse stringers. This is followed by an outer layer of solid, ¼" Honduras mahogany planks carefully lined off fore-and-aft and glued down with epoxy. The construction demands care, skill, and high-quality materials. To reduce building time and costs, you might replace the solid mahogany planking with a second skin of plywood—and paint the whole works. But that would violate the spirit, if not the letter, of this plan. We suspect that designer Bassett would be unhappy.

Rascal's lines show a shallow-V hull with deadrise increasing as the bottom sweeps forward to a strong chin. Note the "pad keel"—a flat, horizontal surface that runs along the bottom from Station 2 aft, widening as it approaches the transom. This "water ski" provides dynamic lift to counteract the weight of the driver, engine, and fuel. It allows the boat to jump onto a plane quickly (in four seconds with the suggested engine), and it seems to add stability at high speeds.

We have driven Rascal and found that she carves turns with authority—banking appeared to be less than we might have predicted, but there was no sense of impending tripping. The hull did pound violently when pushed hard into a steep chop, but such carrying-on was clearly outside the design parameters.

In addition to her outstanding performance, Rascal is a striking boat—in, or out of, the water.

Rascal's plans include eight large sheets of drawings: profile and deck plan, lines and offsets, cutaway construction plan, full-sized mold patterns (three sheets), stem and cutwater patterns, and expanded transom. There are 15 sheets of specifications. WB Plan No. 100, $120.00.

Plan 100

DESCRIPTION
Hull type: V-bottomed runabout
Construction: Plywood and mahogany over sawn
  frames
PERFORMANCE
*Suitable for: Protected waters
*Intended capacity: 1–2
  Trailerable: Yes
  Propulsion: 45- to 60-hp outboard engine
  Speed: 52 mph with 60 hp

BUILDING DATA
Skill needed: Intermediate to advanced
Lofting required: No
*Alternative construction: Cold-molded,
  double-laminated plywood
PLANS DATA
No. of sheets: 8
Level of detail: Above average
Cost per set: $120.00
WB Plan No. 100

*See page 96 for further information.

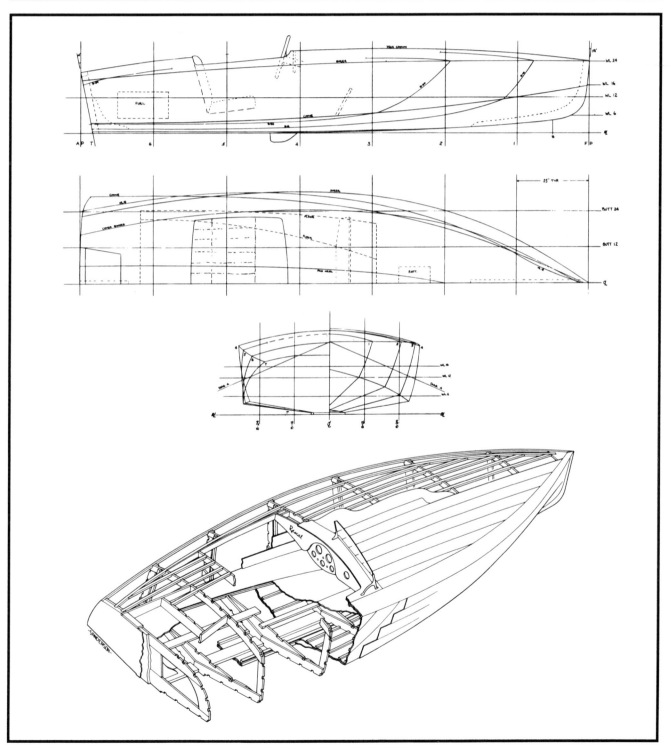

15'9" and 19' Ben Garveys

by Doug Hylan

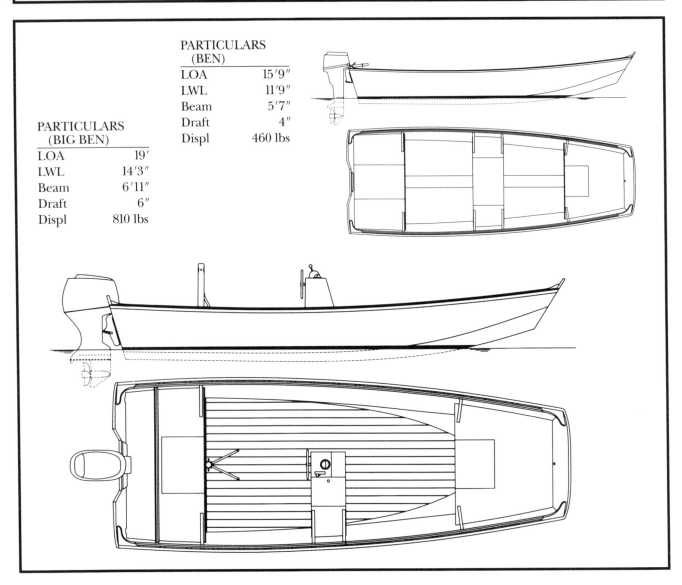

PARTICULARS (BEN)

LOA	15'9"
LWL	11'9"
Beam	5'7"
Draft	4"
Displ	460 lbs

PARTICULARS (BIG BEN)

LOA	19'
LWL	14'3"
Beam	6'11"
Draft	6"
Displ	810 lbs

Here is a pair of boats that will feel right at home on the working waterfront. Both would make fine boatyard skiffs or small harbor-ferries. Both would be fine for a little recreational fishing or getting around the lake on summer vacation, or ferrying out to that island camp. The larger boat would make a fine skiff for some entry-level lobstering or shellfish harvesting.

Garveys originated as shallow-draft, burdensome, and easily built boats for working the shallow bays and estuaries of the Jersey Shore. The advent of the internal-combustion engine, and later, the outboard motor, ensured their survival since the hull form is actually better suited to mechanical power than to the sailing rigs of the early boats. Doug Hylan has refined the Ben garveys somewhat from their original form: They show a strong sheer and more rake to the bow transom for good looks, the buttock lines aft have been straightened out for planing speeds, and the construction is updated to make use of plywood and epoxy. But they still display the same characteristics that made their forefathers popular: ease of construction, shallow draft, good stability, and great load capacity.

You build the Ben garveys of plywood, upside down on a ladder frame over temporary molds. Lofting is required, but it is extremely simple. The chines are easily made using epoxy fillets and fiberglass tape. Flotation compartments ensure that a swamped boat will float level and support the motor head above the water.

The plans are printed on five sheets (four for Big Ben) and include lines, construction, details, and building jig. Also included are instruction sheets that cover tools and materials, scarfing plywood, construction, and use. WB Plan Nos. 126 (BEN) and 127 (BIG BEN), $75.00 each.

Plans 126 and 127

DESCRIPTION
Hull type: V-bottomed garveys
Construction: Plywood planking over bulkheads
PERFORMANCE
*Suitable for: Protected waters (BEN);
  somewhat protected waters (BIG BEN)
*Intended capacity: 1–6 (BEN); 1–8 (BIG BEN)
  Trailerable: Yes
  Propulsion: 15–35 hp (BEN); 25–75 hp (BIG BEN)
  Speed (knots): 15–30

BUILDING DATA
Skill needed: Basic
Lofting required: Yes
*Alternative construction: None
PLANS DATA
No. of sheets: 5 (BEN); 4 (BIG BEN)
Level of detail: Above average
Cost per set: $75.00
WB Plan Nos. 126 (BEN) and 127 (BIG BEN)

*See page 96 for further information.

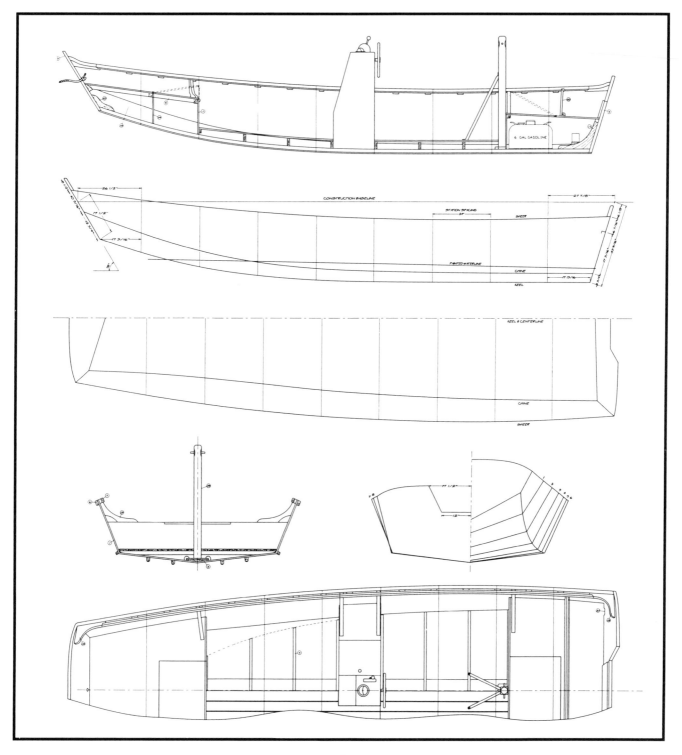

16' San Juan Dory

by David Roberts

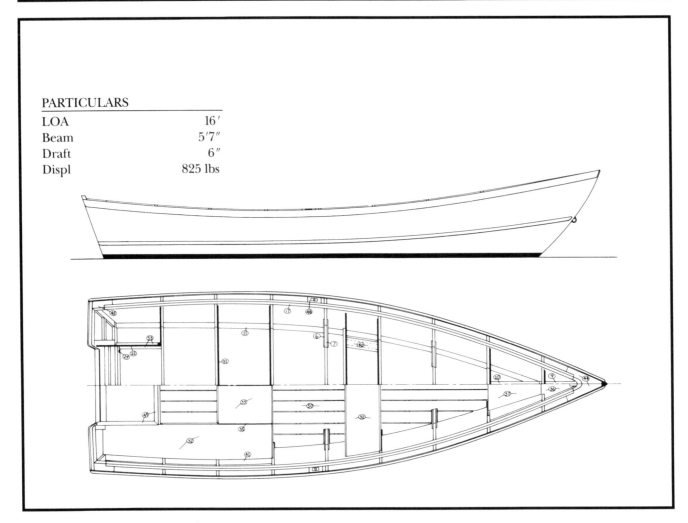

PARTICULARS

LOA	16'
Beam	5'7"
Draft	6"
Displ	825 lbs

This rugged and able 16' outboard-powered dory combines beauty with practicality—and it is easy to build. David Roberts designed the handsome hull and built it as the Nexus 16' Dory. Now, for the first time, this highly regarded builder has been persuaded to offer the original plans for sale.

The high bow and deep sides of this dory will shed rough water and give you a feeling of confidence out of proportion to the hull's length. Go birding in the sloughs, camping on the islands, or salmon fishing in the straits. This boat is up to the job.

The straightforward, traditionally framed, sheet-plywood construction is both educational and simple. And, unlike stitch-and-glue boats, this dory allows you a choice of glues, compounds, and fastenings. Epoxy is great goop, but not every builder can, or wants to, work with it.

You'll make the dory's sides from 6mm plywood and its bottom from 9mm or 10mm plywood. The solid timber for stem, frames, rails, etc., can be oak or mahogany or any acceptable local woods. All of the wood in this boat can be bent into place cold; no steaming or soaking is necessary.

If you wish, the San Juan Dory's bulkheads can be eliminated, resulting in a clear, unobstructed interior. Simply make frames Number 2 through 8 according to the chine-gusset system shown for frame Number 3.

Despite its great strength, this dory weighs only 300 lbs. Motors of 10 hp to 20 hp will move it along at speeds ranging from 12 knots to 18 knots. Although a 20-hp engine is most appropriate, you'll find that a 15-hp engine will provide satisfactory performance; however, a motor of 10 hp will prove marginal at best. Because it is so easily driven, there's no sense in hanging engines of more than 20 hp on this hull.

Styles come and go, but there's always room along the waterfront for rugged, practical boats like this dory. This is a boat you'll keep, not a boat that you'll sell.

The dory's plans include: outboard profile, lines plan, offsets, construction and arrangement plans, and seven pages of specifications. WB Plan No. 123, $75.00.

Plan 123

DESCRIPTION
Hull type: Flat-bottomed
Construction: Plywood planking over sawn frames

PERFORMANCE
*Suitable for: Somewhat protected waters
*Intended capacity: 1–6
Trailerable: Yes
Propulsion: 15- to 20-hp outboard
Speed (knots): 12 to 18

BUILDING DATA
Skill needed: Basic to intermediate
Lofting required: Yes
*Alternative construction: None

PLANS DATA
No. of sheets: 3
Level of detail: Average
Cost per set: $75.00
WB Plan No. 123

*See page 96 for further information.

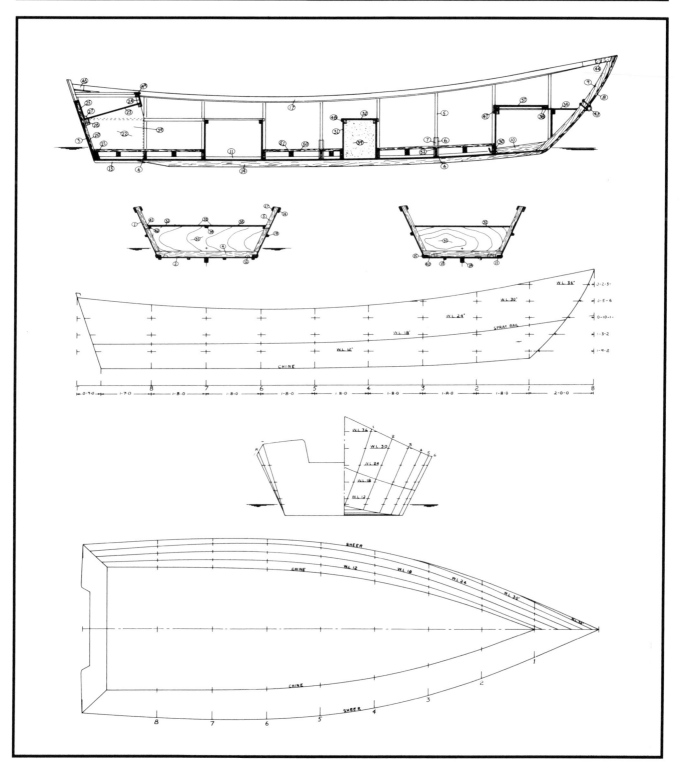

18'6" Outboard Skiff Cruiser, Redwing

by Karl Stambaugh

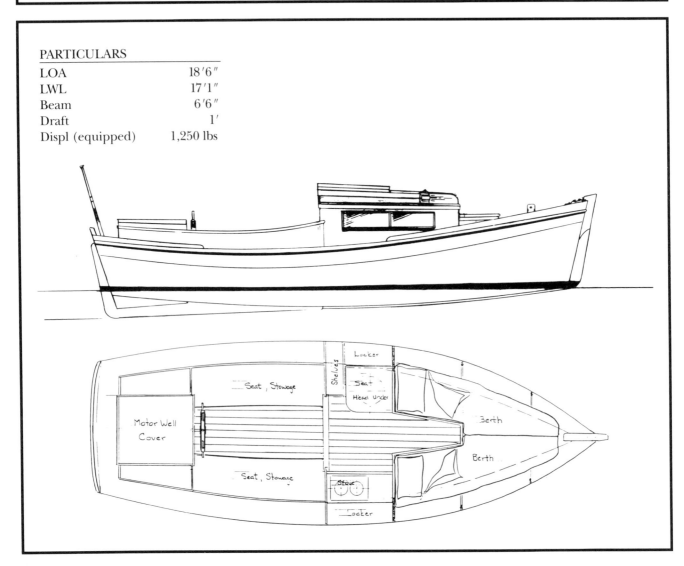

PARTICULARS

LOA	18'6"
LWL	17'1"
Beam	6'6"
Draft	1'
Displ (equipped)	1,250 lbs

Inspired by an old Howard Chapelle design (see WB No. 82, page 114), Karl Stambaugh demonstrates that we need not mimic the short, fat, and inefficient stock outboard cruisers of the 1950s.

Redwing's nicely proportioned hull will be easily driven at moderate speeds in more or less protected waters. Although 5 hp will do the job, a 10-hp, four-cycle outboard would be a nearly perfect (if somewhat expensive) match. Quiet, dependable, and economical of fuel, these motors are loved by all who own them. To reduce noise, Stambaugh drew an insulated motorwell. We suspect you'll hear the hiss of the bow wave during lulls in conversation. As with all motorwells, you should provide adequate ventilation and check that the well's dimensions will permit your motor to tilt up fully.

Unlike the traditional skiff construction specified by Chapelle, Stambaugh calls for sheet plywood and epoxy.

Short of being holed, a hull built to these plans has no excuse for leaking a single drop, ever—a desirable characteristic, as bilgewater in flat-bottomed boats soon invades the accommodations. And Redwing's plywood hull can live happily on a trailer.

Stambaugh's drawings are filled with worthwhile details. For example, he shows a drip groove routed into the bottom of the rubrails. Gravity and surface tension will cause water flowing from the deck to drop from the rails at the groove rather than running down, and staining, the topsides.

Because of her relative silence and sharp control, Redwing will be welcome in most any harbor. But we see her as in the evocative sketch on the title page of this book: pressing far upstream past the cattails.

Redwing's plans contain ten sheets, including the arrangement plan, hull lines and offsets, and construction drawings. WB Plan No. 108, $90.00.

Plan 108

DESCRIPTION
Hull type: Flat-bottomed
Construction: Plywood planking over sawn frames
Headroom/cabin (between beams): About 3'6"

PERFORMANCE
*Suitable for: Protected waters
*Intended capacity: 1–4 day tripping, 2 cruising
Trailerable: Yes
Propulsion: 5–10 hp outboard engine
Speed (knots): Up to 6

BUILDING DATA
Skill needed: Intermediate
Lofting required: Yes
*Alternative construction: stitch and glue

PLANS DATA
No. of sheets: 10
Level of detail: Average
Cost per set: $90.00
WB Plan No. 108

*plans include stitch and glue details

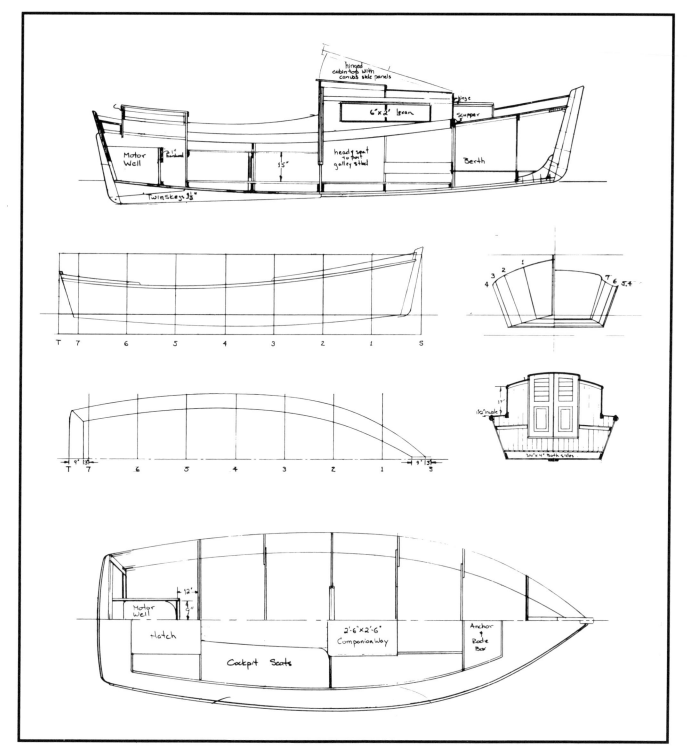

19'9" Runabout

by the Albury Brothers/plans by Doug Hylan

PARTICULARS

LOA	19'9"
LWL	17'8"
Beam	6'10"
Draft	1'1"
Displ	2,400 lbs

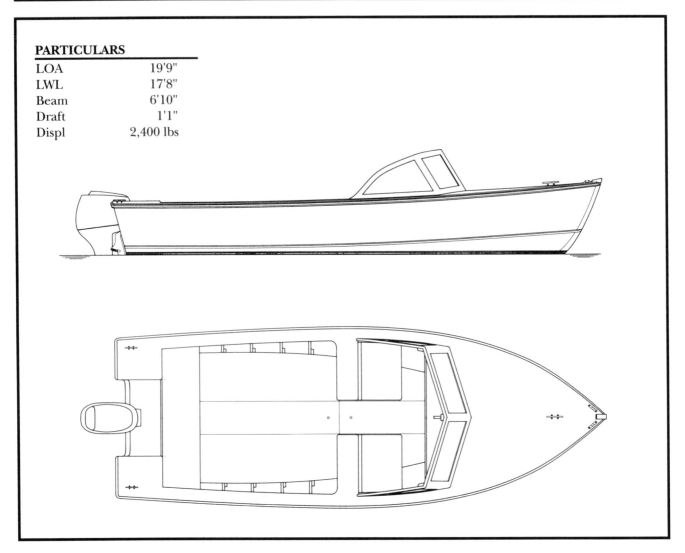

In the northern Bahamas, the Albury name is synonymous with boatbuilding. For generations, this family has turned out hundreds of boats, from dinghies to schooners, from their building sheds on Man O' War Cay in the Abacos. Since the mid-1950s Willard and Benny Albury have been producing fine outboard runabouts that have earned a reputation as smooth-riding, seaworthy, rugged boats, capable of excellent speed with modest horsepower.

For many years, these boats were built in wood, by eye, with no two boats being exactly alike. After building so many unique variations on a single boat type, the Albury brothers have a pretty good idea of the important factors in runabout design. The plans shown here represent what Willard Albury considers to be his optimal boat, the best of over 250 individual boats.

Doug Hylan has drawn a set of plans that not only document the construction of these fine boats, but make it

possible for other builders to enjoy their good qualities. The lines show a moderate deadrise of 15 degrees with a fine entry, producing an easy ride even in the short, steep chop common in the shallow waters of the Bahamas. Construction is robust but simple and clean, making these boats long-lived and easy to maintain.

The Albury runabout will make a fine project for intermediate and advanced builders. Glued strip planking over frames sawn from natural Madeira root knees was the original construction, but most builders today will probably find it easier to laminate their frames. For those who would prefer cold-molding, a construction sheet is included for this method. Lofting is required, but this is not a difficult set of lines to lay down.

Six sheets of plans show lines, original construction, cold-molded construction, and details. Calculations for U.S. Coast Guard safe powering, load capacity, and flotation requirements are included. WB Plan No. 136, $90.00.

Plan 136

DESCRIPTION
Hull type: V-bottomed runabout
Construction: Strip-planked over laminated frames
PERFORMANCE
*Suitable for: Somewhat protected waters
*Intended capacity: 1–7 day cruising
Trailerable: Yes
Propulsion: 40–120 hp outboard engine
Speed (knots): 22–44 mph
BUILDING DATA
Skill needed: Intermediate to advanced

Lofting required: Yes
*Alternative construction: Cold-molded, plans
  included
PLANS DATA
No. of sheets: 6
Level of detail: Above average
Cost per set: $90.00
WB Plan No. 136

See page 96 for further information.

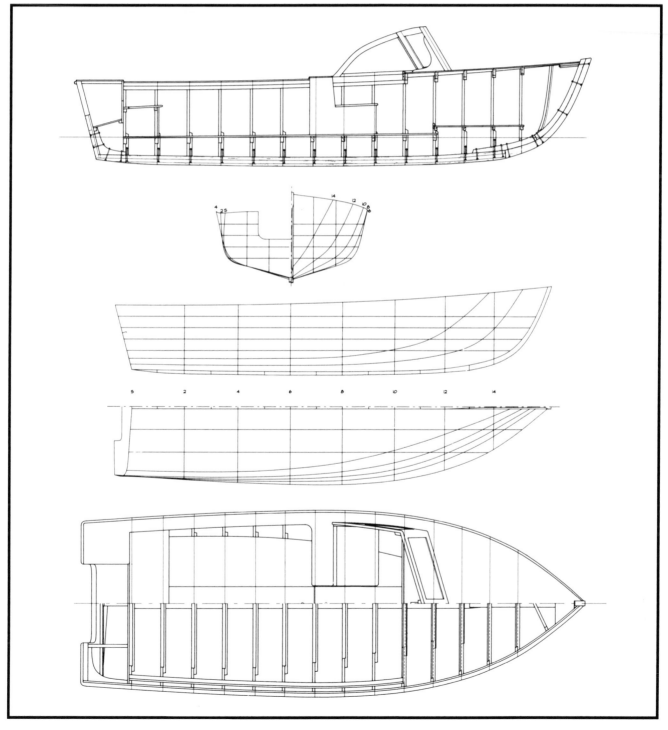

—59—

20' Utility Launch

by Eliot Spalding

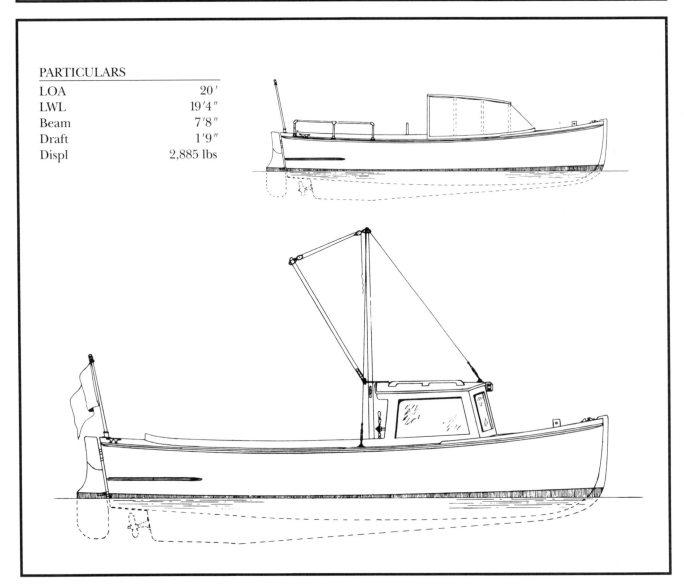

PARTICULARS	
LOA	20'
LWL	19'4"
Beam	7'8"
Draft	1'9"
Displ	2,885 lbs

Most small powerboats these days are designed for high speeds, and if you need to get there in a hurry, they can do it. But if you are going out on the water for pleasure, why not slow down and enjoy yourself? You'll see the scenery in more detail, save yourself and the world a little fuel and pollution, and be a lot more likely to receive a friendly wave from other folks out on the water.

Here is a rugged little launch that will remind many of the Hampton boats that used to be such a common feature of the waterfront years ago. These were fine craft that successfully made the transition from sail to power, combining the good load-carrying and seakeeping abilities of their sailing ancestors with healthy speeds made possible by engines of modest horsepower available at the time.

Eliot Spalding has drawn this boat with generous beam, so she'll have lots of room and stability. Her construction features a traditional bolted-up backbone of oak, steam-bent frames, and strip planking, but there is no reason she couldn't be carvel planked. For that matter, her lines would lend themselves to cold-molding or glued-lap plywood if the builder wanted to make the conversion.

Four different arrangements are shown: two versions with cabins, an open launch with a canvas shelter, and a spritsail-rigged version that might be useful so long as your destination is downwind. This is a semi-displacement boat, designed to operate at speeds between 8 and 10 knots, and a more powerful engine than the Westerbeke 4-91 shown will result in very little more speed.

These plans are drawn for the builder with some experience, and are printed on seven sheets, including lines, construction, and four arrangements. WB Plan No. 124, $120.00.

Plan 124

DESCRIPTION
Hull type: Round-bottomed
Rig: Sprit
Construction: Strip-planked over steam-bent frames

PERFORMANCE
*Suitable for: Somewhat protected waters
*Intended capacity: 1–6 day cruising
Trailerable: Yes
Propulsion: Inboard gas or diesel
Speed (knots): Up to 10

BUILDING DATA
Skill needed: Intermediate to advanced
Lofting required: Yes
*Alternative construction: Carvel, cold-molded,
  glued-lapstrake plywood

PLANS DATA
No. of sheets: 7
Level of detail: Average
Cost per set: $120.00
WB Plan No. 124

See page 96 for further information.

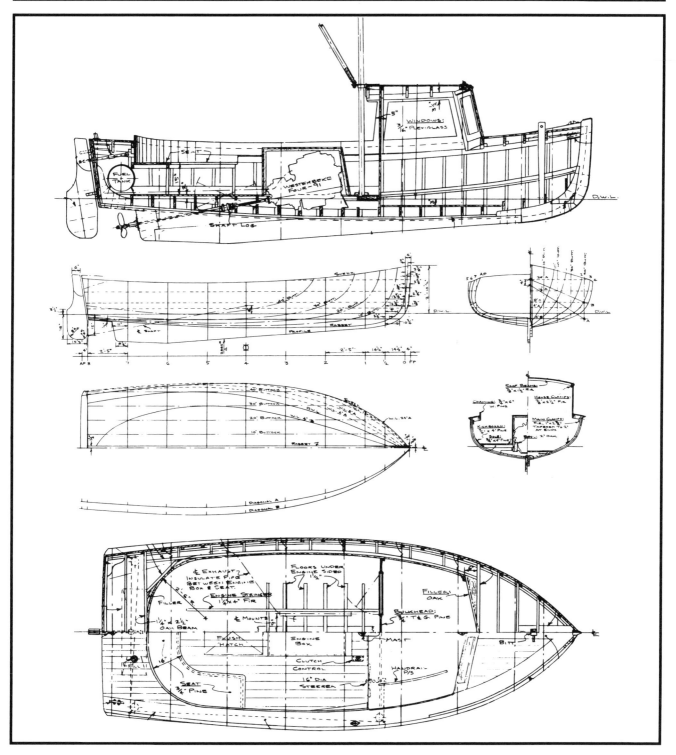

—61—

22' Palm Beach and Newport Runabouts

by Nelson Zimmer

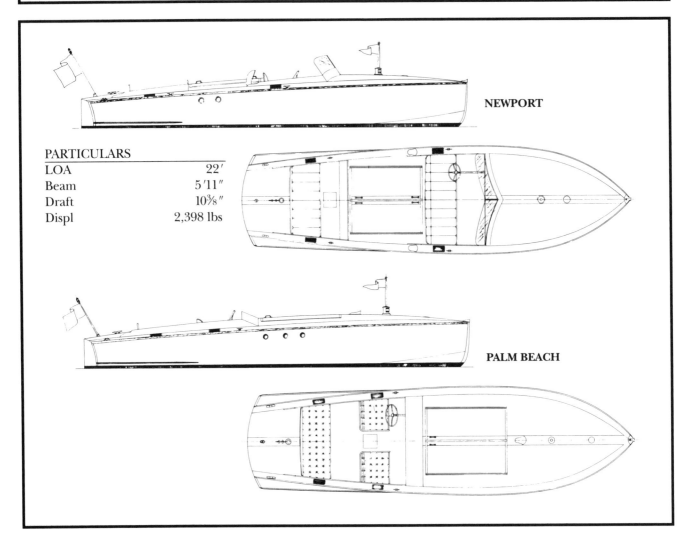

NEWPORT

PALM BEACH

PARTICULARS	
LOA	22'
Beam	5'11"
Draft	10⅜"
Displ	2,398 lbs

Despite the proliferation of deep-V "cigarette" boats during the last few decades, the classic mahogany runabouts of the 1920s and '30s continue to attract new admirers. It's a matter of style.

The warm glow of a carefully varnished hull and deck can make you believe that the finish is three feet deep. And few experiences on the water can match hunkering down in a deep cockpit and feeling the neck-bending acceleration provided by a large-displacement engine.

The above opinions enjoy sufficient popularity along the waterfront to ensure the future value of classically styled runabouts. Indeed, these boats can prove to be handsome investments. But simple and easy construction is not one of their virtues. They demand flawless workmanship from their builders. Every cut and every fit will provide expert craftsmen with opportunities to demonstrate their skills.

Their hard chines notwithstanding, these hulls won't accept sheet-plywood panels. First, you'll erect a substantial skeleton of white oak and/or ash. Then, cut-in notches for the battens that back up each plank seam. Bottom planking is ⁹⁄₁₆" mahogany. Topside planks will be ½" mahogany. Decking is specified to be ⅜" mahogany or white pine with ³⁄₃₂" seams lightly caulked with cotton and payed with compound of contrasting color. Of course, you'll want to display all of this under at least 10 coats of carefully applied varnish.

The hulls for the single-cockpit Palm Beach and the split-cockpit Newport are identical. They will trim properly at the designed waterline with an engine weighing 675 lbs. An engine of that weight, which produces 150 hp, will push either boat to about 45 mph. A 250-hp engine, weighing in at 740 lbs, should give a top speed of about 55 mph. And the boats will look fine at any speed.

Plans for the Palm Beach and Newport runabouts are available separately, and each plans set consists of four sheets that include profile and arrangement, lines and offsets, construction details, and hardware/fittings. WB Plans 98 (Palm Beach) and 99 (Newport), $120.00 for each set.

Plans 98 and 99

DESCRIPTION
Hull type: V-bottomed runabout
Construction: Battened-seam planking over sawn
 frames
PERFORMANCE
*Suitable for: Protected waters
*Intended capacity: 1–4
Trailerable: Yes
Propulsion: 150-hp inboard gasoline engine
Speed: 45 mph

BUILDING DATA
Skill needed: Advanced
Lofting required: Yes
*Alternative construction: None
PLANS DATA
No. of sheets: 4
Level of detail: Average
Cost per set: $120.00 each
WB Plan Nos. 98 (Palm Beach) and 99 (Newport)

*See page 96 for further information.

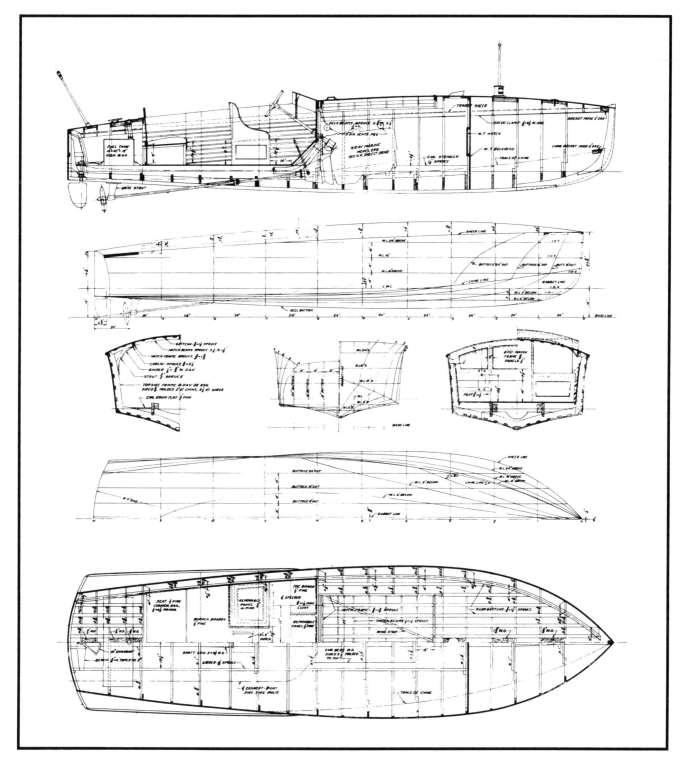

28′ Bermuda Runabout

by Nelson Zimmer

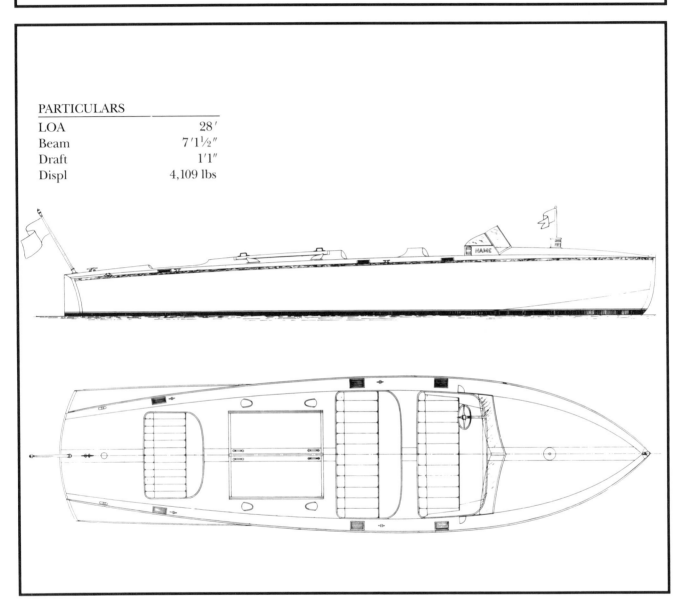

PARTICULARS	
LOA	28′
Beam	7′1½″
Draft	1′1″
Displ	4,109 lbs

Here's one for the dedicated runabout enthusiast. Measuring a full 28′ in length, and capable of 50 mph when powered with a 300-hp engine, the Bermuda offers all of the thrust and thunder you might want.

As with Bermuda's smaller cousins, the 22′ Palm Beach and Newport, this big hull is copiously framed and heavily planked to withstand the tremendous stresses imparted by high speed. The main frames (of ash or white oak) are sided ¾″ and molded 3″. Bottom planking is specified to be ¾″ mahogany on seam battens or a layer of ½″ mahogany over two layers of ⅛″ cedar laid diagonally. The deck is planked with 6½″-wide, ½″-thick mahogany; and a false seam is to be worked down the center of each strake. Finally, everything will need to be covered with several coats of the finest varnish you can find.

Period hardware and fittings will provide a good part of the ambiance aboard this runabout. If you're not an experienced hand in the foundry and machine shop, the search for a reputable professional firm with compassion for your project should begin before you lay Bermuda's keel.

Designer Nelson Zimmer was a close friend and informal associate of John Hacker, the legendary master of runabout design. The touch of Hacker's ideas is evident in the subtle curves of Bermuda's hull lines and correctness of the detailing. Everything is in its place, and everything is as it should be.

Plans for Bermuda consist of three sheets and include profile and arrangement, lines and offsets, and construction details. There are five pages of specifications. WB Plan No. 105, $120.00.

Plan 105

DESCRIPTION
Hull type: V-bottomed runabout
Construction: Battened-seam planking over sawn frames

PERFORMANCE
*Suitable for: Protected waters
*Intended capacity: 1–6
Trailerable: Yes
Propulsion: 300-hp inboard engine
Speed: 50 mph

BUILDING DATA
Skill needed: Advanced
Lofting required: Yes
*Alternative construction: None

PLANS DATA
No. of sheets: 3
Level of detail: Average
Cost per set: $120.00
WB Plan No. 105

See page 96 for further information.

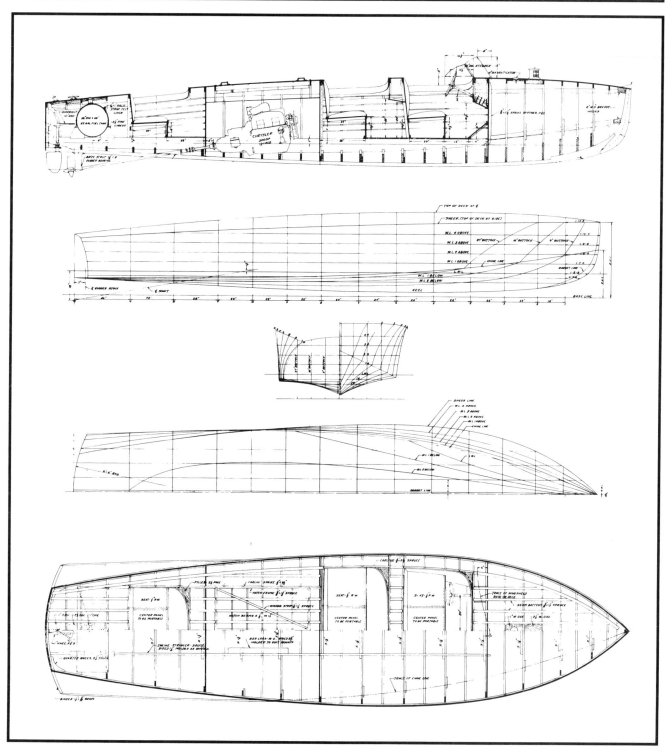

19' Cat Schooner, BOAT

by William Garden

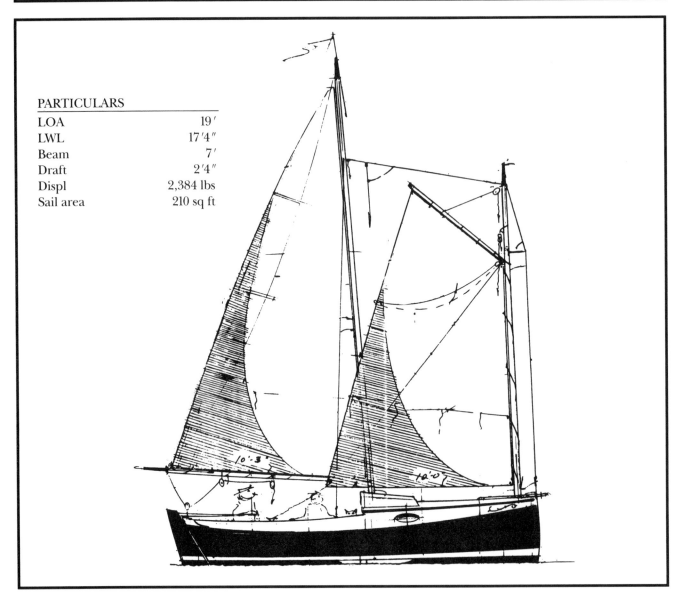

PARTICULARS	
LOA	19'
LWL	17'4"
Beam	7'
Draft	2'4"
Displ	2,384 lbs
Sail area	210 sq ft

While many young sailors get their start in small one-design racing classes, some kids are born cruisers, with more of Tom Sawyer than Dennis Conner in their blood. These youngsters may not have the bankroll or the instincts to succeed on the race course, but might be dreaming of a bit of longer-range adventure, perhaps spending the night with a buddy in that little cove a mile or two away. Often these dreamers would have the gumption to forsake the TV and build for themselves the vessel of their dreams, if they had a bit of encouragement.

Certainly, Bill Garden was such a youngster, and he has not forgotten the call of those boyhood sirens. BOAT is the latest in a long series of refinements to Bill's idea of the perfect kid's cruising boat. Simple enough to be put together in the garage, salty enough to build a daydream on, BOAT is also safe enough so that loved ones left ashore will be able to sleep as well as those aboard. Of course, the young in years are not the only ones who will love this one—anyone who is young at heart can enjoy her simple charms.

BOAT's plywood-over-sawn frame construction is straightforward and should not prove beyond the abilities of anyone with a little woodworking experience and the enthusiasm to see a project like this through. Young builders will probably need more than just encouragement, but can you think of a finer thing for a parent (or grandparent) than to help a young cruiser build and sail BOAT?

BOAT's plans are on six sheets, and include lines, sail and deck plan, and construction plan with lots of large-scale cross sections to clarify details. WB Plan No. 130, $100.00.

Plan 130

DESCRIPTION
Hull type: Double-ended, finkeel
Rig: Cat schooner
Construction: Plywood planking over sawn frames
Headroom/cabin (between beams): About 3'5"
PERFORMANCE
*Suitable for: Somewhat protected waters
*Intended capacity: 1–4 daysailing, 2 cruising
Trailerable: Yes
Propulsion: Sail w/inboard auxiliary

BUILDING DATA
Skill needed: Intermediate
Lofting required: Yes
*Alternative construction: None
PLANS DATA
No. of sheets: 6
Level of detail: Average
Cost per set: $100.00
WB Plan No. 130

See page 96 for further information.

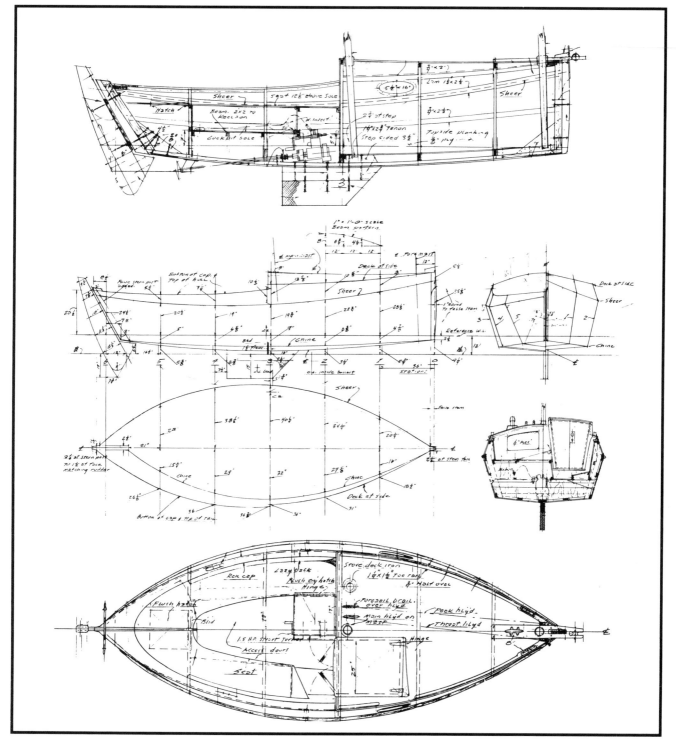

19'6" Sloop Mist

by Karl Stambaugh

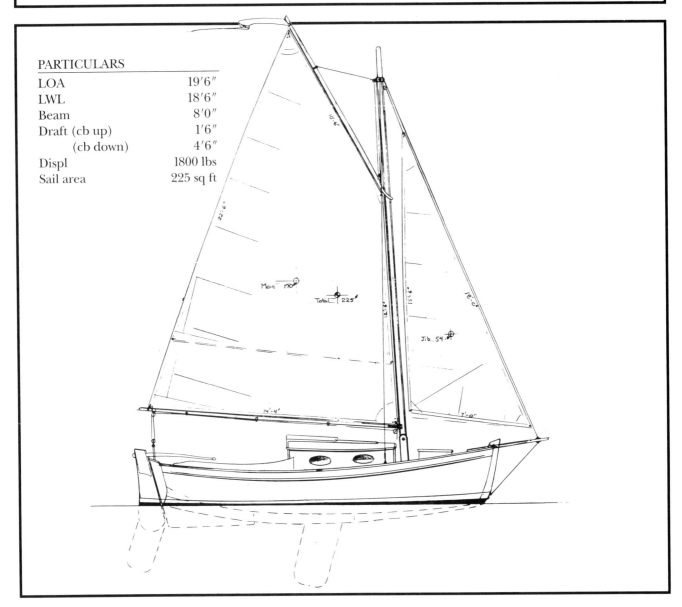

PARTICULARS

LOA	19'6"
LWL	18'6"
Beam	8'0"
Draft (cb up)	1'6"
(cb down)	4'6"
Displ	1800 lbs
Sail area	225 sq ft

Designer Karl Stambaugh has gone out of his way to ensure that this plywood pocket cruiser doesn't look like a plywood boat. He drew the stem to stand proud, as it would on a conventionally planked hull. Solid, coved sheerstrakes add to the illusion, as does the severe rounding-over specified for the chines. And the curved, raked transom isn't exactly standard fare for sheet-plywood boats. In all, this is a handsome little cruiser.

In some ways, Mist awakens old memories of the plywood sloops that filled the pages of Popular Whatever magazines in the years following World War II. Down below, the designer made no attempt to cram in coffin-like quarter berths or an enclosed head. (There is no such thing as privacy aboard a 20' boat in any case.) Mist's arrangement is simple and traditional, and it works fine. The relatively wide cabin sole survives the intrusion of the long center-board trunk (part of which hides under the bridge deck).

Mist's cockpit offers comfortable lounging space, but this will be slightly degraded if you build the optional outboard motorwell. You might consider hanging a removable bracket to the transom or after deck. Better yet, investigate the mysteries of the yuloh (an efficient, curved sculling oar).

With her handsome style, and easily stepped mast (mounted in a tabernacle so that it can pivot up and down for trailering or low bridges), Mist might be the ideal trailerable cruiser.

Mist's plans contain six sheets: general information, lines and offsets, construction drawings, construction details, surfaces, and sail plans (gaff-rigged sloop and optional gunter-rigged sloop). WB Plan No. 107, $90.00.

Plan 107

DESCRIPTION
Hull type: V-bottomed, centerboard boat
Rig: Gaff- or gunter-rigged sloop
Construction: Plywood planking over sawn frames
Headroom/cabin (between beams): About 4'2"
Featured in WB No. 107
PERFORMANCE
*Suitable for: Somewhat protected waters
*Intended capacity: 1–4 daysailing, 2 cruising
Trailerable: Yes

Propulsion: Sail w/outboard auxiliary
BUILDING DATA
Skill needed: Intermediate to advanced
Lofting required: Yes
*Alternative construction: None
PLANS DATA
No. of sheets: 6
Level of detail: Average
Cost per set: $90.00
WB Plan No. 107

See page 96 for further information.

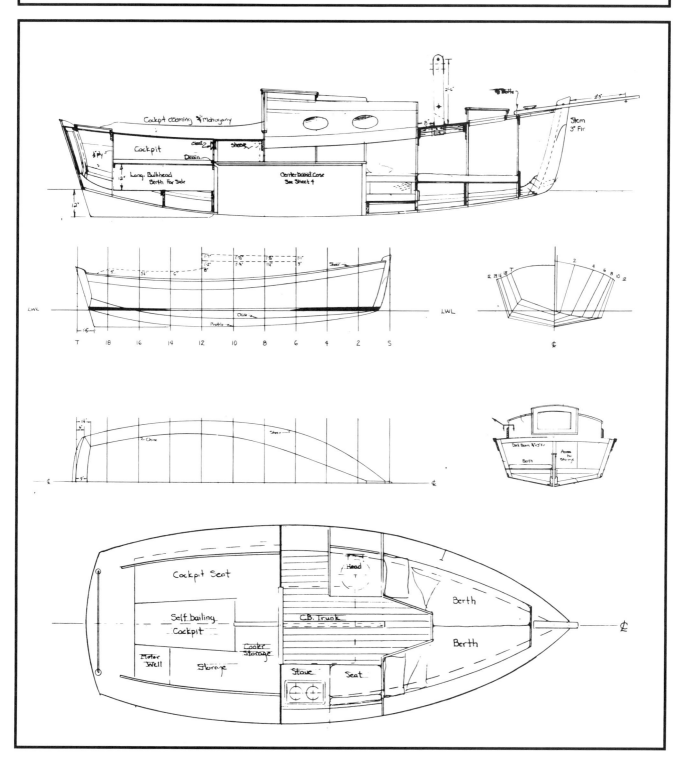

20'4" Sloop, Maid of Endor

by John Atkin

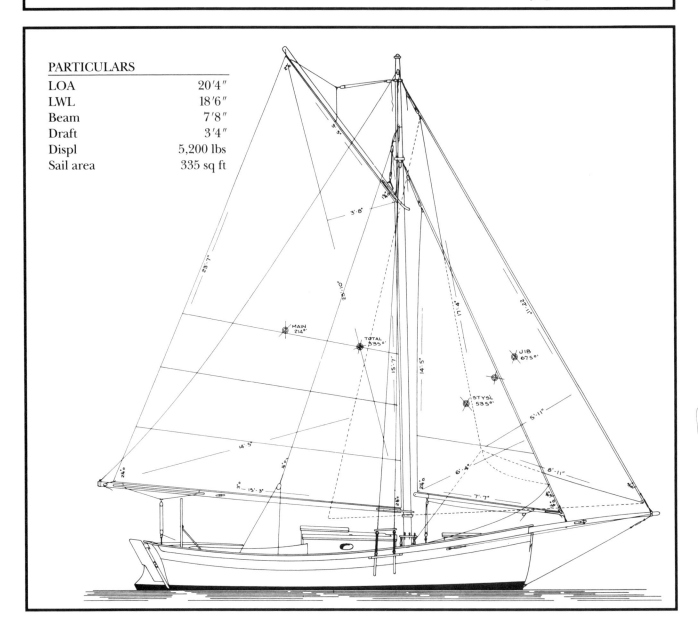

PARTICULARS

LOA	20'4"
LWL	18'6"
Beam	7'8"
Draft	3'4"
Displ	5,200 lbs
Sail area	335 sq ft

Here we have a 20' sloop that seems as right-of-line as any classic design. Maid of Endor will prove challenging to build, but she'll reward your efforts with incomparable charm and grace. According to designer John Atkin, the seed for this hull's lovely shape came from larger vessels that fished the coast of Brittany. They were, he wrote, "long proven for their seakeeping ability and swiftness under sail."

An abundance of shape and flare above her waterline give Maid of Endor a light and airy appearance that belies her 5,200 lbs displacement. When she's under sail, relatively firm bilges help make finding the "groove" an easy job. She puts her shoulder down, only so far, and moves on. Her bow wave rolls aft in a handsome curl, and she leaves little fuss behind. This little packet foots well; and

she'll get to windward in fine fashion, for her type—if you don't strap her down too hard.

Atkin specifies traditional plank-on-frame construction for Maid of Endor. Built to the plans, she'll show plenty of satisfying structure down below. The peace of mind this provides for her crew shouldn't be underestimated.

By contemporary standards, Maid of Endor represents a heavy and expensive way to move two berths and a snug cockpit around the bay. But she is so lovely. How can we put a price on her elegance?

The plans for Maid of Endor consist of five sheets of drawings: the sail plan (suitable for framing), lines plan, table of offsets, hull construction, and arrangement. WB Plan No. 133, $120.00.

Plan 133

DESCRIPTION
Hull type: Round-bottomed, outside-ballasted keel boat
Rig: Gaff sloop
Construction: Carvel-planked over steamed frames
Headroom/cabin (between beams): About 3'10"
Featured in WB Nos. 22, 59

PERFORMANCE
*Suitable for: Open ocean
*Intended capacity: 1–4 daysailing, 2 cruising
Trailerable: Yes

Propulsion: Sail w/inboard auxiliary

BUILDING DATA
Skill needed: Advanced
Lofting required: Yes
*Alternative construction: Cold-molded, strip

PLANS DATA
No. of sheets: 5
Level of detail: Below average
Cost per set: $120.00
WB Plan No. 133

*See page 96 for further information.

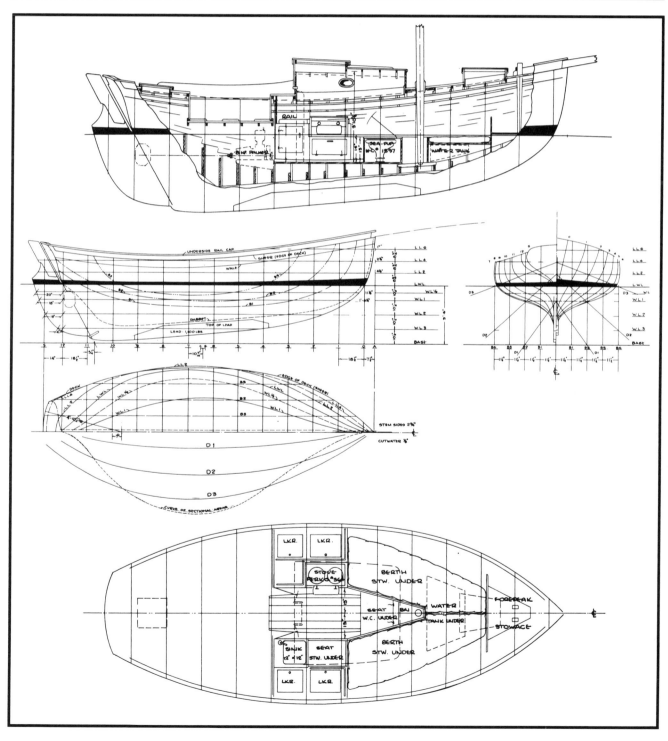

24' Open/Cruising Boat Paketi

by David Payne

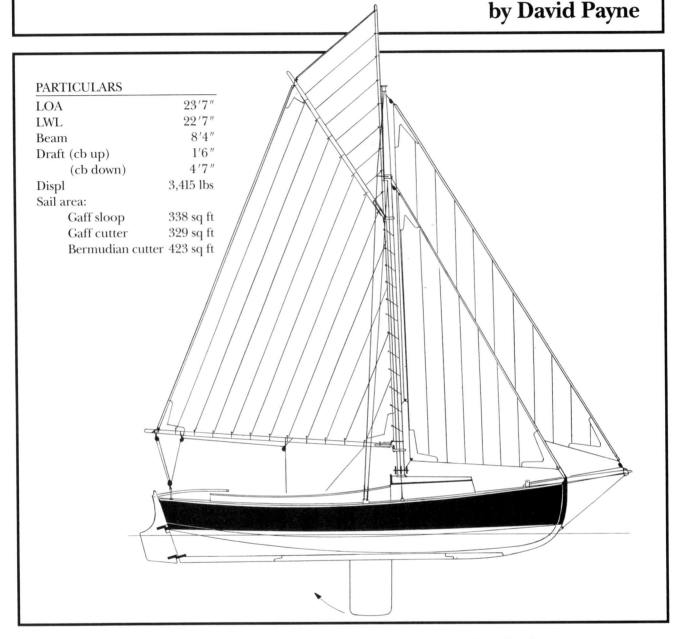

PARTICULARS

LOA	23'7"
LWL	22'7"
Beam	8'4"
Draft (cb up)	1'6"
(cb down)	4'7"
Displ	3,415 lbs
Sail area:	
Gaff sloop	338 sq ft
Gaff cutter	329 sq ft
Bermudian cutter	423 sq ft

In Paketi, Australian designer David Payne has given us a handsome, easily constructed boat with lots of possibilities. Originally drawn as an open-cockpit daysailer and camp cruiser, the design has sparked so much interest that two cabin versions have been added. There are choices in rig as well. For those unromantic enough to prefer simple efficiency, the marconi cutter will be just the thing. But, a shipload of young pirates might appreciate the gaff rig, with a string or two for each crew member. In light airs, setting the topsail will add another challenge.

With a board-up draft of only 18", Paketi will have nothing to fear from thin water. In fact, if your cruising grounds feature warm water and protected beaches, you might dispense with a dinghy. The ballast shoe will add comforting stability, and well-flared topsides contribute reserve buoyancy and good looks.

Lofting Paketi's single-chine hull will be very simple. Construction is plywood planking over sawn frames and stringers—a simple, straightforward system with a well-proven track record. Her ballast casting and outboard rudder are both easily constructed. In short, building Paketi should not prove beyond the abilities of anyone with a little woodworking experience and some perseverance. Paketi's plans are dimensioned in the metric system, but this shouldn't scare you off—just get a metric tape measure. After you've used this system for a while, especially for lofting, you may understand why the rest of the world has switched over.

Paketi's well-detailed plans are on eight sheets, including lines, construction, two sail plans, and details. WB Plan No. 112, $175.00.

Plan 112

DESCRIPTION
Hull type: V-bottomed keel/centerboard boat
Rig: Sloop or cutter
Construction: Plywood planking over sawn frames
Headroom/cabin (between beams): About 4'8" in
  motorsailer
PERFORMANCE
*Suitable for: Somewhat protected waters
*Intended capacity: 1–5 daysailing; 2 cruising
 Trailerable: Yes, permit required

Propulsion: Sail w/outboard auxiliary
BUILDING DATA
Skill needed: Intermediate to advanced
Lofting required: Yes
*Alternative construction: Strip
PLANS DATA
No. of sheets: 8
Level of detail: Average
Cost per set: $175.00
WB Plan No. 112

See page 96 for further information.

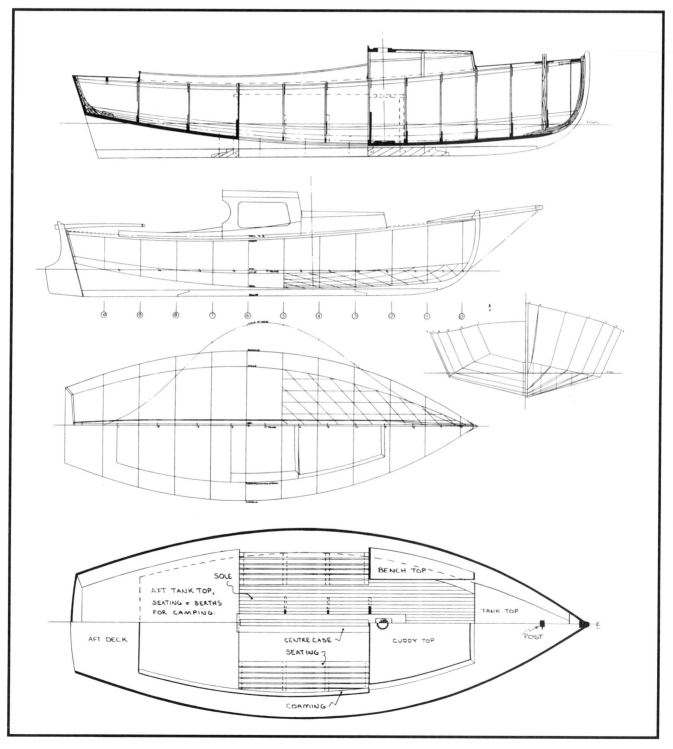

25'9" Lubec Boat

by Brewer, Wallstrom & Assoc.

PARTICULARS

LOA	25'9"
LWL	22'6"
Beam	8'9"
Draft	4'
Displ	11,500 lbs
Sail area	460 sq ft

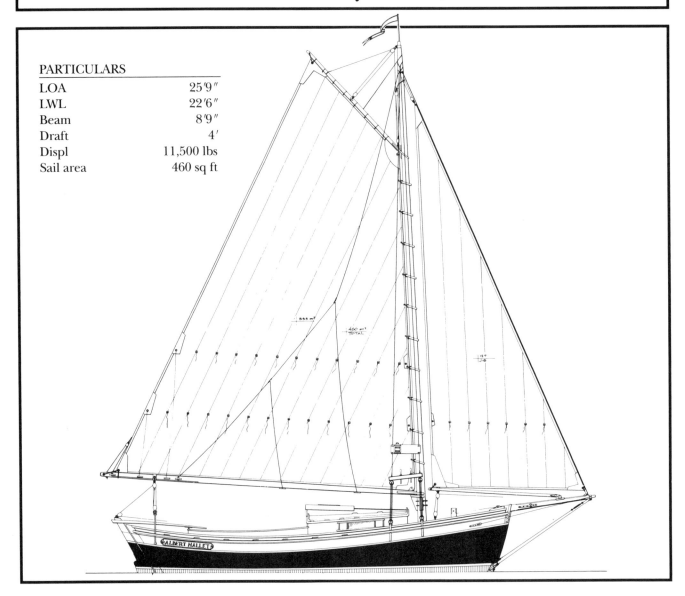

Right where the great Passamaquoddy Bay empties into the even mightier Bay of Fundy, is Lubec, Maine, the easternmost spot in the United States. This is a land of swirling currents, confounding fogs, and canny fishermen. Not that long ago, it was also the home waters of the incredibly able Lubec boat, a double-ender legendary for its seakeeping abilities.

Ted Brewer and Bob Wallstrom drew the Lubec Boat for Penobscot Boat Works, as a smaller sister to their well-regarded 32' Quoddy Pilot. Here is a pocket cruiser more salty than a barrel of slack-salted cod, and if the thought of mast hoops, deadeyes, and pine tar brings a lump to your throat, this could be just the packet for you. Her generous sail plan will keep her going in light airs, but if the tide is getting the best of you, just fire up the iron breeze and be home in time for chowder. And despite her small size, you won't have to worry if a little nasty weather catches you out.

The plans provide something unusual for a boat of this type—not just lines and a few construction sketches, but very complete drawings covering everything from backbone to masthead. The technology is decidedly low key (strip-planking with concrete and steel inside ballast), but not necessarily old school (plywood decks, laminated keel and stem). There are detailed hardware drawings, lots of construction details, and a very complete list of specifications. And don't let lofting scare you off; WB No. 12 has a detailed article on lofting the Lubec Boat. Yes, a builder with a little experience and a lot of gumption could build this boat.

Plans are printed on twelve sheets and include lines, construction, joiner sections, sail and spar plans, and mast hardware. WB Plan No. 116, $210.00.

Plan 116

DESCRIPTION
Hull type: Round-bottomed, keel boat
Rig: Gaff sloop
Construction: Strip-planked over steam-bent frames
Headroom/cabin (between beams): About 5′6″
PERFORMANCE
*Suitable for: Open ocean
*Intended capacity: 1–6 daysailing, 2 cruising
Trailerable: With difficulty, permit required
Propulsion: Sail w/inboard auxiliary
BUILDING DATA
Skill needed: Intermediate to advanced

Lofting required: Yes
*Alternative construction: Carvel, cold-molded
Helpful information: "Lofting the Lubec Boat," by
  Sam Manning, WB No. 12
PLANS DATA
No. of sheets: 12
Level of detail: Above average
Cost per set: $210.00
WB Plan No. 116

*See page 96 for further information.

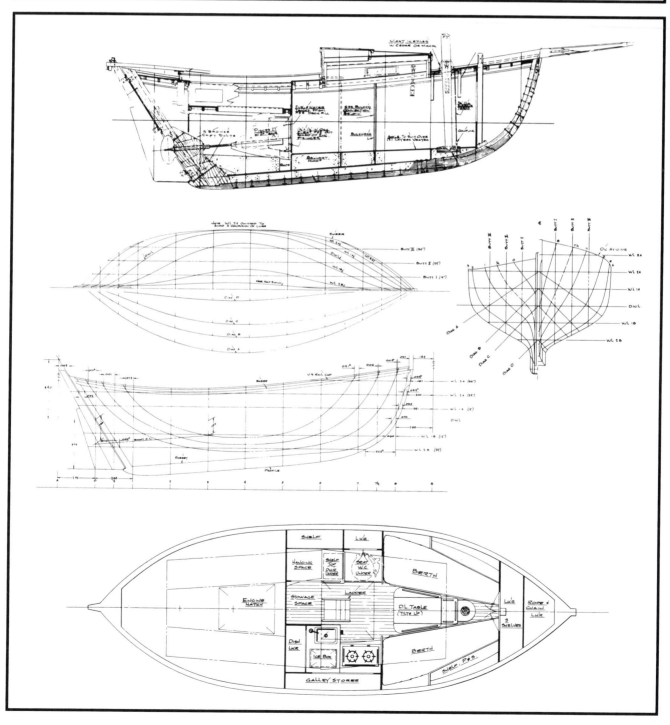

28' Canoe Yawl, Rozinante
by L.F. Herreshoff/Modifications by D.N. Hylan

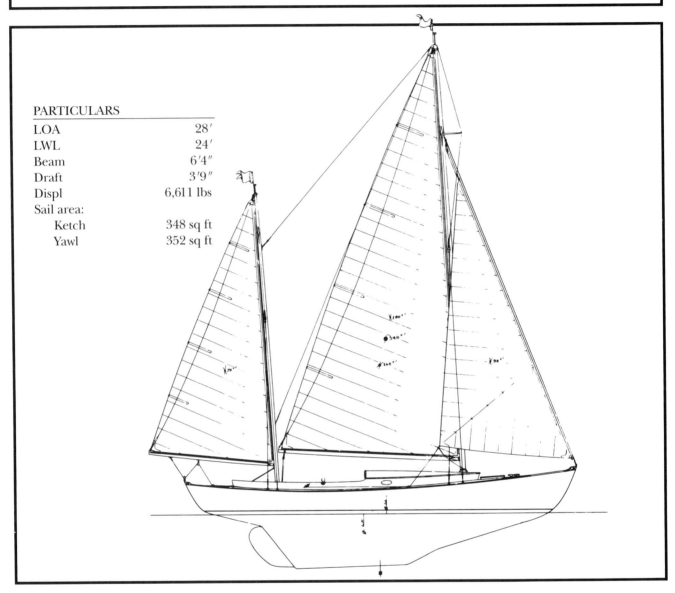

PARTICULARS

LOA	28'
LWL	24'
Beam	6'4"
Draft	3'9"
Displ	6,611 lbs
Sail area:	
Ketch	348 sq ft
Yawl	352 sq ft

In the midst of the dark years of World War II, *The Rudder* magazine commissioned L. Francis Herreshoff to write a how-to-build article for a design that would give war-weary sailors something to dream about until life could return to normal. In fact, this article became the first of a series that lasted right through the mid-'50s and has become the foundation of several books. In the last articles of the series, as well as in his book *The Compleat Cruiser*, Herreshoff introduces us to Rozinante, a "light-displacement canoe yawl."

Rozinante embodies many of L.F.H.'s well-distilled ideas on what cruising should be about—simplicity, beauty, peace of mind. Without an engine, a boat can be more of a challenge to a sailor's skill but, at the same time, a visual and auditory relief. Although she is not an easy boat to build, Rozinante offers the satisfaction of working with

natural materials and using time-honored techniques to produce an object as lovely in the shop as on the water.

WoodenBoat is proud to be able to offer what must certainly be one of the most exquisite designs ever to come from the drawing board. "Herreshoff's dainty canoe yawl has power beyond her apparent delicacy, ability beyond her size, and elegance beyond her cost," says Roger Taylor in WB No. 26. Phil Bolger describes Rozinante as "hypnotically beautiful" and possessed of "thoroughbred manners" in his biography of L.F.H. (WB No. 56).

Rozinante's plans are printed on nine sheets, including Herreshoff's original lines, construction, sail, spar, and rigging plans. Also included are three drawings by Doug Hylan showing an updated construction plan as well as sail and spar plans for a yawl-rigged version (see WB No. 123). WB Plan No. 134, $325.00.

Plan 134

DESCRIPTION

Hull type: Round-bottomed, double-ended keel boat
Rig: Ketch or yawl
Construction: Carvel-planked over steam-bent frames
Headroom/cabin (between beams): About 4'4"
Featured in WB Nos. 26, 123

PERFORMANCE

*Suitable for: Somewhat protected waters
*Intended capacity: 1–6 daysailing; 2 cruising
Trailerable: With difficulty

Propulsion: Sail

BUILDING DATA

Skill needed: Advanced
Lofting required: Yes
*Alternative construction: Cold-molded

PLANS DATA

No. of sheets: 9
Level of detail: Above average
Cost per set: $325.00
WB Plan No. 134

See page 96 for further information.

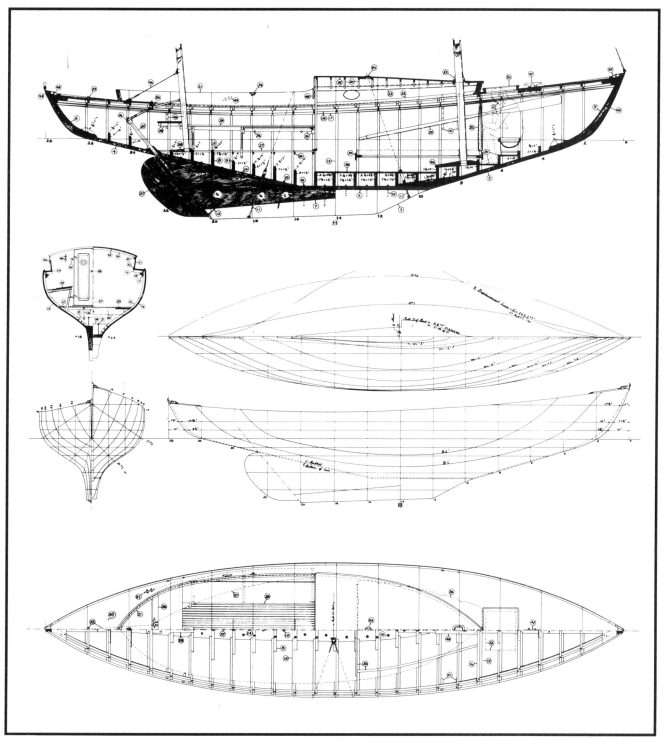

32' Mystic Sharpie

by Edward S. Brewer

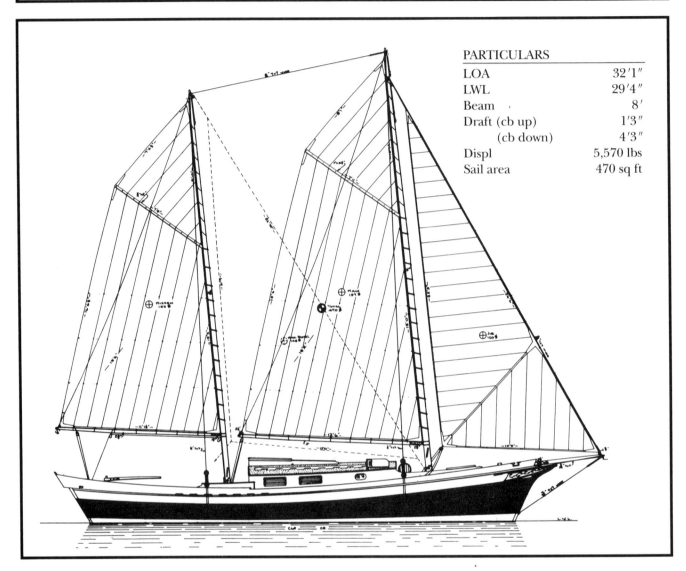

PARTICULARS	
LOA	32'1"
LWL	29'4"
Beam	8'
Draft (cb up)	1'3"
(cb down)	4'3"
Displ	5,570 lbs
Sail area	470 sq ft

Ted Brewer drew this 32' double-ended sharpie ketch to provide the amateur builder with a shoal-draft cruising boat of simple construction and low cost.

Mystic's low and powerful sail plan is carried by simple spruce masts (solid or hollow, at the builder's option). This rig, which resembles a gaff ketch with topsails, comes from the Great Lakes working sharpies. But, close inspection of Brewer's drawings reveals that the mainsail and its "topsail" are, in fact, of one stitched-together piece, as is all the canvas set on the mizzenmast. The "gaffs" consist of ¾ × 2" battens placed on each side of the sails and riveted directly through the sailcloth.

With her outside lead ballast, self-bailing cockpit, and ample freeboard, Mystic is a safer rough-water boat than the old low-sided, half-decked working sharpies. For this sharpie's robust construction, Brewer specifies a 1¼"-thick bottom (laminated from two or three layers of sheet ply-

wood). The topsides consist of a single or double layer of plywood to finish at ⅝" in thickness.

The accommodations provide four full-sized berths, generous storage space, and complete facilities for extended cruising. Brewer has worked the requisite large centerboard trunk into the main cabin without totally bisecting the accommodations. A dropleaf table hangs from the after portion of the trunk.

Mystic retains all the advantages of the original working sharpies: her shoal draft allows her to cross bars and explore gunkholes that are forbidden to keelboats; she handles easily; and she's easily built, yet capable of coastwise cruising.

Mystic's plans contain four sheets of drawings: sail plan, hull lines and offsets, construction and arrangement, and miscellaneous details. There are 11 pages of specifications. WB Plan No. 122, $195.00.

Plan 122

DESCRIPTION
Hull type: Flat-bottomed centerboard sharpie
Rig: Gaff ketch
Construction: Plywood planking over sawn frames
Headroom/cabin (between beams): About 4'6"

PERFORMANCE
*Suitable for: Somewhat protected waters
*Intended capacity: 1–6 daysailing, 4 cruising
Trailerable: Yes
Propulsion: Sail w/outboard auxiliary

BUILDING DATA
Skill needed: Intermediate
Lofting required: Yes
*Alternative construction: None

PLANS DATA
No. of sheets: 4
Level of detail: Average
Cost per set: $295.00
WB Plan No. 122

*See page 96 for further information.

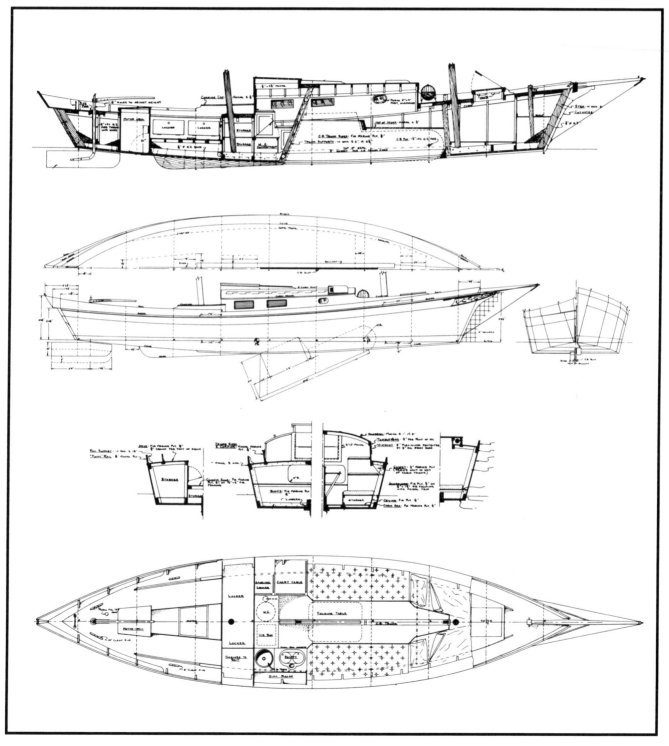

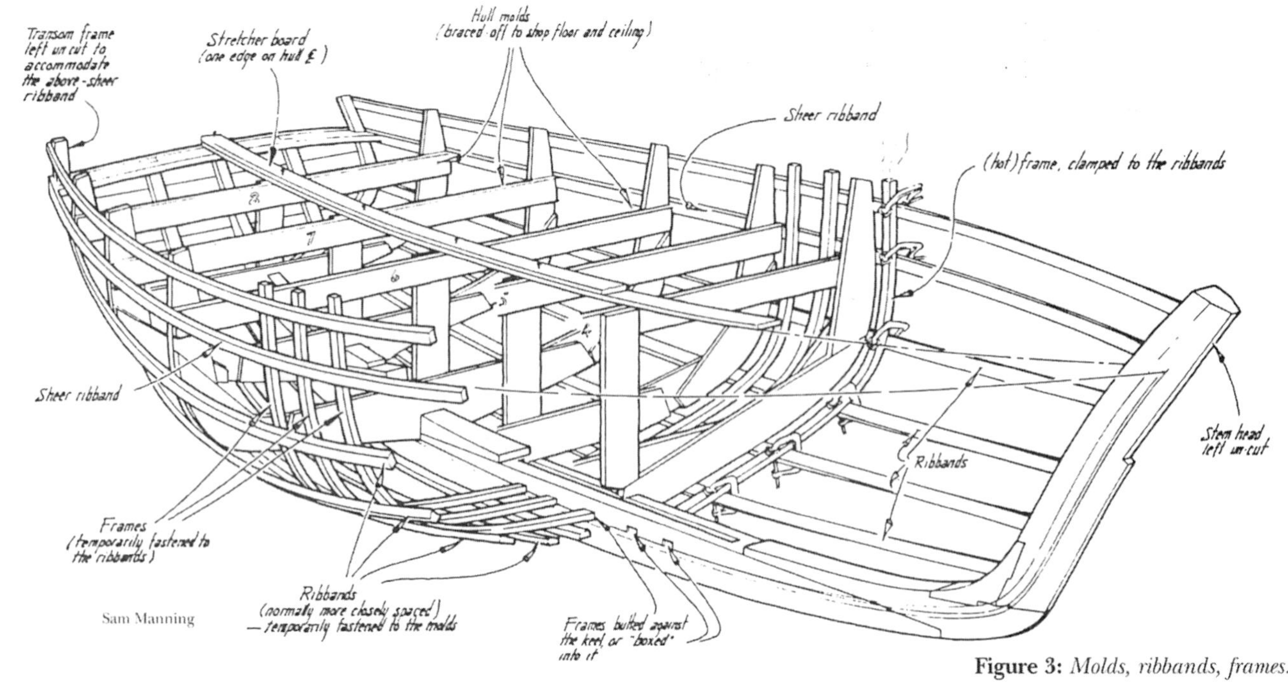
Transom frame left un-cut to accommodate the above-sheer ribband
Stretcher board (one edge on hull ℄)
Hull molds (braced off to shop floor and ceiling)
Sheer ribband
(hot) frame, clamped to the ribbands
Sheer ribband
Stem head left un-cut
Ribbands
Frames (temporarily fastened to the ribbands)
Ribbands (normally more closely spaced) —temporarily fastened to the molds
Frames butted against the keel or "boxed" into it

Sam Manning

Figure 3: *Molds, ribbands, frames.*

Continued from page 7

I would suggest ordering a piece 5″ thick by 9″ wide and 10′long. Notice that this piece is the same size as the piece we ordered for the stem and knees. This will give us some flexibility in layout of the patterns, and the ability to choose the best piece of wood for the stem. Tell your sawmill that, as much as possible, you would like these backbone pieces to be clear of the heart of the tree. This may not be possible in all cases—large-dimensioned keels usually have to include the heart simply because big-enough logs are not available to saw such a keel clear of the heart.

While we are still thinking in terms of oak needed for this vessel, let's try to figure what else we must order.

Frames

The specifications call for 1¼″-square steam-bent frames. The longest of these need to be about 6′, and there are 24 pairs or 48 individual pieces needed. Figure 10% extra for breakage, although with good oak and good steam you should actually break only two or three pieces; 10% brings your total up to 53 pieces. The oak will have to be ⁶⁄₄ in order to plane down to 1¼″ thickness. Figure on ripping the stock into 1½″-wide blanks; ¼″ for the saw kerf makes 1¾″, plus a little leeway for other milling losses brings you up to 2″. The square footage per piece is 2″ divided by 12 times 6′ (length) equals 1 square foot per piece times 53 equals 53 square feet times ⁶⁄₄ equals 80 board feet. Knowing how aggravating it is to come up a couple of frames short, I would order 100 board feet of green, clear, oak bending stock in 12′ lengths. The length is important—if the mill gives you a lot of your bending oak in 8′ or 14′ lengths, it may not cut to advantage, and you will end up short of timbers. The best rule with bending stock is to order more than enough. When you are sawing out the stock, if you reach your count before reaching the end of the pile, fine—you can use the remainder elsewhere in the boat. If you don't order enough, you may not have anything else suitable for bending. While air-dried oak will bend if properly steamed, green oak is much the best, and there will be less breakage. I would not order live-edge (flitch-sawn) lumber for frames, as there is too much wastage and extra work involved in milling out the pieces. The best use for flitch-sawn lumber is for the heavy backbone timber, or for long pieces such as the clamps which need a fair amount of sweep, and for cedar planking. Cedar often grows with a sweep, which can be used to advantage when getting out planks.

Cabinsides and Coamings

Looking through the specifications for this little boat, the other items that call for steam-bent oak are the round cabinsides and coamings. Two pieces of ¼ × 12″ × 16′clear bending stock will be needed for these and should be specified on the order. They will be butted on the centerline forward. Clear pieces of this size may be hard to find today, and when we built the boat 20 years ago, we laminated the house sides out of thin plywood.

Go through the specifications carefully, listing each item calling for oak, note the thickness required, and figure the square feet of lumber needed to get out all the pieces. Multiply the square feet by the thickness to get the board feet required.

Deckbeams

For example, the four heavy deckbeams finish 1¾″ in thickness and are about 6′in length. Their molded depth finishes 1¾″ and, because of the crown, will require about 5″ of width to saw out. But one can usually lay out two or three beams per plank, crown inside of crown, and thus minimize waste. Figuring to cut to 2″ molded before dressing to 1¾″, the square footage per beam is 2″ divided by 12 times 6 (feet of length) equals 1 square foot per beam times ⁸⁄₄ equals 2 board feet per beam times four beams equals 8 board feet, total. I would double this to allow for waste; thus, these four beams require 16 board feet of ⁸⁄₄

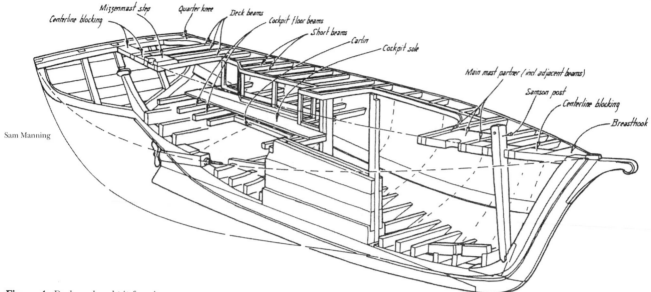

Figure 4: *Deck and cockpit framing.*

oak. The other items that require ⁵⁄₄ oak are a few pieces of deck blocking, the breasthook, and the two centerboard posts. Another 8 board feet will supply these items; thus your lumber list should include 25 board feet ⁵⁄₄ RWL oak.

The items listed in the specifications that call for ⁶⁄₄ oak are the floor timbers, stern framing, bilge stringers, clamps, and rudder. I won't detail the calculation for each of these items, as this article would soon be too boring to read. But let's just run through one for practice.

Floor Timbers

Take the floor timbers: There are 21 shown on the drawings, the longest ones amidships being about 3′ by 6″ in depth. Floor timbers are roughly trapezoidal in shape, and, by flipping your patterns, you can cut them to good advantage from your stock. Let's say the average floor timber will be 2′ long by 6″ in depth, or 1 square foot per timber times 21 equals 21 square feet times ⁶⁄₄ equals 33 board feet. Add 25% for waste—or, say, 42 board feet total.

Following the same procedure, I arrive at 10 board feet for stern framing, 20 bf for bilge stringers, 25 bf for clamps, and 20 bf for the rudder. These numbers include a factor for waste which varies with the item involved. Bilge stringers can be sawn out straight and may only need 10% extra for waste; clamps have a lot of shape that must be sawn into them and may need 30% for waste. Adding up the board feet, including our 42 bf for the floor timbers, we need 117 bf of ⁶⁄₄ RWL oak for all items. Round it up to 125 bf, and add it to the list.

Butt blocks, ordinary deckbeams, toerails, cockpit floorbeams, and the centerboard all come out of ³⁄₄ oak. Performing the same calculations, I arrive at 90 bf of ³⁄₄ RWL oak to swell out the list.

For the housetop beams, which are ⅞″ × 1¼″, we need ¼ oak. Fifteen bf will do, but there are sure to be a number of small items we will want to cut from this useful thickness—cleats, bits of trim, moldings, etc. So add 25 bf ¼

RWL oak to the list, and we have completed the oak requirements.

Planking

The next major item of lumber needed is planking, which is specified to be cedar to finish 1″. Calculate the square feet needed by multiplying the length of the boat (20′) by the maximum girth (both sides) amidships (10′), or 200 square feet. Add 20 square feet for the transom. You will need ⁵⁄₄ cedar to plane up 1″ net, so 220 times ⁵⁄₄ equals 275. There is a lot of waste in planking because no plank is a straight board, so I usually allow 50% more, which comes to 413 board feet; 425 bf of ⁵⁄₄ live-edge (flitch-sawn) cedar goes on the list. Do not plane all your planking stock to 1″ thickness, as you will need thicker pieces at the turn of the bilge where the planks must be hollowed to fit the frames. Save out 25–30% of your plank stock, and leave it at ⁵⁄₄ thickness.

Centerboard Trunk Sides

The sides of the centerboard trunk are specified as 1¼″ white pine, splined and glued. Each side is about 2′ wide and 5′ long. I would use five pieces of stock about 5″ wide to plank up the trunk each side, so five planks ⁵⁄₄ × 6″ × 10′ will do nicely. The trimmings after milling the pieces should suffice for the splines.

Hull Ceiling

We ceiled the hull inside from the bow to the main bulkhead with ⁵⁄₁₆″ pine. The area will be about 4′ × 12′ each side, or 96 square feet total. Four-quarter pine boards can be resawn and planed to ⁵⁄₁₆″ thickness, so about 50 board feet plus 15% for waste, or 60 board feet total, will do.

Plywood Requirements

The deck is specified as ½″ marine plywood. The best way to estimate the plywood needed for this job is to cut

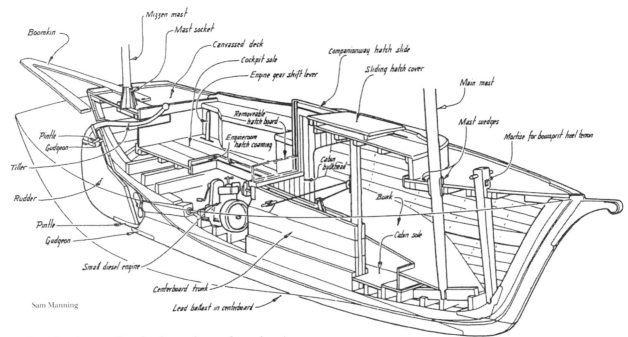

Figure 5: *Centerboard case, ceiling, hatches, and masts for yawl version.*

Labels on figure:
Boomkin — Mizzen mast — Mast socket — Canvassed deck — Cockpit sole — Engine gear shift lever — Companionway hatch slide — Sliding hatch cover — Main mast — Mast wedges — Mortise for bowsprit heel tenon — Removeable hatch board — Engineroom hatch coaming — Cabin bulkhead — Pintle — Gudgeon — Tiller — Rudder — Pintle — Gudgeon — Bunk — Cabin sole — Small diesel engine — Centerboard trunk — Lead ballast in centerboard — Sam Manning

out a paper $4 \times 8'$ panel to the scale of the plans, and actually lay out the arrangement of the panels on the deck plan. Upon doing this, you will learn that by having a butt joint between deckbeams near Station 3 and a fore-and-aft seam on the centerline, the entire forward deck (both sides) can be cut from one sheet of plywood. Two sheets will cover the after part of the boat from the stern forward to about Station 5½, and the trimmings from the cockpit area will fill in the side deck remaining between Stations 3 and 5½. One sheet will make the cockpit floor. So, four sheets of ½" AA marine fir plywood will cover the deck and the cockpit. The main-cabin bulkhead also requires one sheet of ½" plywood. There should be enough extra plywood after the pieces are cut to provide for the butt blocks needed under the seams in the deck plywood. Below, we used two sheets of ⅜" plywood to build a seat bunk on each side. The cabintop is specified as ½" plywood. I was worried that it would be difficult to accommodate the extra crown with plywood this thick, and used two layers of ¼" with the joints staggered. Again using your scale $4 \times 8'$ paper panel, you can determine that four sheets of ¼" AA marine fir will be needed to make both layers.

Spars

Next, let's consider the spars. The specifications call for Sitka spruce, with the mainmast being a hollow box section, the booms and bowsprit of solid spruce. As it happened, I was able to obtain good, clear, local white spruce from my nearby building-supply contractor at a much lower price than Sitka, so we used this for the spars. In any case, the mast is glued up from ¹³⁄₁₆" and ⁹⁄₁₆" staves, which must be gotten out of ¼ stock. The mast length is 28'2" overall. It is doubtful that you will be able to obtain 29' pieces, even in Sitka, so there will probably have to be a scarf joint in each of the four staves, well scattered throughout the length of the spar. You will need 120 lineal feet (30' × 4), plus another 10 lineal feet for the four scarfs, or a total of

130 lineal feet of ¼ × 4", or 65 lineal feet of ¼ × 8". Ask your lumber dealer for the longest lengths he has, which will give the most flexibility as to the placement of the scarfs. The main boom is a solid piece $2\frac{5}{32}" \times 3\frac{5}{32}"$ at its greatest section, and 14'2" long; so one piece of ¹²⁄₄ × 4" × 16' will do—or, if ¹²⁄₄ is not available, two pieces of ⁶⁄₄ × 4" × 16' glued together. For the jib club, which is $2\frac{5}{32}" \times 1\frac{3}{8}"$ in section and 8'4" long, a single piece of ⁶⁄₄ × 4" × 10' spruce will do nicely. The bowsprit finishes a full 2" in thickness, 7" in width, and nearly 7' long; so one piece of ¹⁰⁄₄ × 8" × 8' will be required. The boomkin is of two pieces about 5' long, and will require a ⁶⁄₄ × 4" × 10' plank.

Molds and Ribbands

One item of lumber not yet mentioned that will be needed early on in the building process is the stock required for molds and ribbands. While these do not end up as permanent parts of the finished boat, they are important to the building of it, and must be provided for in your lumber list. Molds are usually made from softwood, such as pine or spruce, but do not require such high-quality material as do the parts of the actual boat. Ribbands are often spruce, or fir, or any reasonably clear wood that comes in long lengths and will bend in true curves. For the molds of this boat, of which there are eight, 1" or 1⅛" stock will be suitable. Wide material is better than narrow for making molds, as the considerable curvature of the sections can be handled with fewer individual pieces per mold. I normally order 9"- or 10"-wide stock for molds, of native spruce, and order enough for both molds and ribbands. When the material comes, I pick out the clearest for ribbands, and use the poorer, knotty pieces for moldmaking. You will also need enough material for a cross spall for each mold, and material to cleat the molds together (see Figure 6). With a scale rule, you can determine that an average mold will require about 12 lineal feet of material, or a total of eight pieces of $\frac{3}{4} \times 9'' \times 12'$ spruce for all molds. Splitting a 9" board in two will give two pieces wide enough for cross spalls. These will need to vary in length from 3' to 8', but let's order two pieces of the same stuff for spalls, and three pieces for cleats, making five more pieces, for a total of 13. You will need about nine ribbands the full length of the boat on each side (one should be above the sheerline), or 18 total. Then, 18 times 20' (length of the boat) equals 360 lineal feet of ribband stock, plus 2 more feet on each ribband for a splice piece adds another 36 lineal feet. Call it 400 lineal feet. You will be able to rip four pieces nearly 2" wide from each 9"-wide board, and so you will need about 100 (400 divided by 4) lineal feet of $\frac{3}{4} \times 9''$ stock. Ask that at least some of this be 14' or 16' long, so that the butts in the ribbands don't all fall in the same place in the length of the boat. So we have arrived at a total of 13 pieces of $\frac{3}{4} \times 9'' \times 12'$ for molds, spalls, and cleats, plus six or seven pieces of the same stuff 16' long to make our 100 lineal feet of ribband stock.

We have now completed our list of lumber needed to construct this simple little boat, with the exception of a few minor items such as cabin floorboards, companionway hatch, cockpit hatch, etc. In a plain boat with an all-paint finish such as this one, there is a good chance that there will be sufficient overage in such items as cedar planking to supply your needs for such items. On a larger boat with a lot of bright-finished parts, your list will be longer, more varied, and will no doubt include some more exotic woods, such as Honduras mahogany for varnished trim parts, perhaps teak for decking or soles, and much more stock needed for interior finishing of the cabin. But the process is the same as detailed here: Estimate the board footage required of the various thicknesses and widths, and from this develop an itemized materials list. The rest is up to your lumber suppliers.

To complete the exercise, let's list the stock we have itemized, by species, by thickness, and by the quantities required—in other words, write out our lumber list. Using LM for local mills, BS for building-supply outlets, and D for lumber dealers, I have indicated the most likely source for each item.

This article originally appeared in WoodenBoat *No. 87.*

Lumber List
20' Crocker Sloop Design No. 300

White Oak
LM 1 piece 8" × 9" × 16' live edge (keel)
LM 2 pieces 5" × 9" × 10' live edge (stem, stem knee, and gammon knee, and centerboard logs and bitt)
LM 1 piece 7½" × 8" × 12' live edge (forefoot, after deadwood)
LM 1 piece 7" × 7" × 8' live edge (shaftlog, horn timber, stern knee)
LM 100 board feet $\frac{3}{4}$ × random square edge × 12' green, clear bending stock (frames)
LM 2 pieces $\frac{1}{4}$ × 12" × 16' green, clear bending stock (cabinsides)
LM 25 board feet $\frac{3}{4}$ RWL (heavy beams, breasthook, centerboard posts)
LM 125 board feet $\frac{6}{4}$ RWL (floor timbers, stern framing, bilge stringers, clamps, rudder)
LM 90 board feet $\frac{7}{8}$ RWL (butt blocks, ordinary deckbeams, toerails, cockpit floorbeams, centerboard)
LM 25 board feet $\frac{1}{4}$ RWL (house beams, trim, moldings, etc.)

Northern White Cedar
LM 425 board feet $\frac{3}{4}$ live edge, long as possible (planking)

Plywood
D 5 sheets ½" AA marine fir (deck, cockpit, bulkhead)
D 2 sheets ⅜" AA marine fir (seat bunks)
D 4 sheets ¼" AA marine fir (cabintop)

Sitka Spruce
D 130 lineal feet $\frac{1}{4}$ × 4" longest lengths available (mast)
D 1 piece $\frac{12}{4}$ × 4" × 16' or 2 pcs. $\frac{6}{4}$ × 4" × 16' (boom)
D 1 piece $\frac{6}{4}$ × 4" × 10' (jib club)
D 1 piece $\frac{10}{4}$ × 8" × 8' (bowsprit)
D 1 piece $\frac{6}{4}$ × 4" × 10' (boomkin)

Native Spruce
BS 13 pieces $\frac{3}{4}$ × 9" × 12' (molds)
BS 7 pieces $\frac{3}{4}$ × 9" × 16' (ribbands)

White Pine
LM or BS 5 pieces $\frac{6}{4}$ × 6" × 10' (centerboard trunk sides)
LM or BS 60 board feet $\frac{1}{4}$ RWL (hull ceiling)

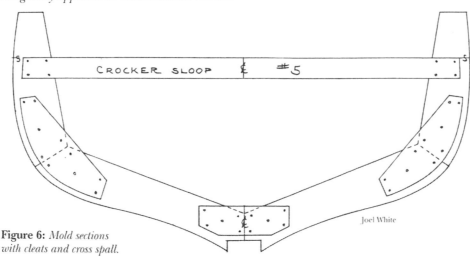

CROCKER SLOOP   # 5

Joel White

Figure 6: *Mold sections with cleats and cross spall.*

Suggested Reading

The best way to learn boatbuilding is to start building a boat. Books and articles can help. They can keep you from entering the blind alleys that have trapped many of us, and they can show you several different paths to the same seaworthy results.

The following titles have been selected for their well-illustrated details and sound technical information. Further description of most of the books listed below, as well as information about back issues of *WoodenBoat* magazine, may be found in the current WoodenBoat Catalog, which is available on request from : WoodenBoat, P.O. Box 78, Brooklin, ME 04616.

Books

Bingham, Fred P. *Boat Joinery & Cabinetmaking Simplified.* Camden, ME: International Marine, 1993.

Bray, Maynard. *How to Build the Haven 12-1/2 Footer.* Brooklin, ME: WoodenBoat Publications, Inc., 1987.

Brewer, Ted. *Understanding Boat Design,* 4th Edition. Camden, ME: International Marine, 1994.

Buehler, George. *Buehler's Backyard Boatbuilding.* Camden, ME: International Marine, 1991.

Calder, Nigel. *Boatowner's Mechanical and Electrical Manual.* Camden, ME: International Marine, 1990.

Chapelle, Howard I. *Boatbuilding.* New York: W.W. Norton & Co., 1994.

Dow, Eric. *How to Build the Shellback Dinghy.* Brooklin, ME: WoodenBoat Publications, Inc., 1993.

Fine Woodworking Editors. *Fine Woodworking on Bending Wood.* Newtown, CT: The Taunton Press, 1985.

_____. *Fine Woodworking on Finishing and Refinishing.* Newtown, CT: The Taunton Press, 1986.

_____. *Fine Woodworking on Wood and How to Dry It.* Newtown, CT: The Taunton Press, 1986.

Gougeon Brothers. *The Gougeon Brothers on Boat Construction,* 4th Edition. Bay City, MI: Gougeon Bros. Inc., 1985.

Hanna, Jay S. *The Shipcarver's Handbook.* Brooklin, ME: WoodenBoat Publications, Inc., 1988.

Hill, Thomas J. *Ultralight Boatbuilding.* Camden, ME: International Marine, 1987.

Hoadley, R. Bruce. *Understanding Wood.* Newtown, CT: The Taunton Press, 1980.

Kulczycki, Chris. *The Kayak Shop.* Camden, ME: Ragged Mountain Press, 1993.

Leather, John. *Clinker Boatbuilding.* London: Adlard Coles, Ltd., 1973.

Lowell, Royal. *Boatbuilding Down East.* South Portland, ME: Simonton Cove Publishing Co., 1994.

McIntosh, David C. *How to Build a Wooden Boat.* Brooklin, ME: WoodenBoat Publications, Inc., 1987.

Marino, Emiliano. *The Sailmaker's Apprentice.* Camden, ME: International Marine, 1994.

Miller, Hub. *The Laminated Wood Boatbuilder.* Camden, ME: International Marine, 1993.

Nicolson, Ian. *Cold-Moulded and Strip-Planked Wood Boatbuilding.* Dobbs Ferry, NY: Sheridan House, 1991.

Pardey, Larry. *Details of Classic Boat Construction: The Hull.* New York: W.W. Norton & Co., 1991.

Parker, Reuel B. *The New Cold-Molded Boatbuilding.* Camden, ME: International Marine, 1990.

Payson, Harold H. *Keeping the Cutting Edge: Setting and Sharpening Hand and Power Saws.* Brooklin, ME: WoodenBoat Publications, 1983.

Rabl, S.S. *Boatbuilding in Your Own Backyard.* Centreville, MD: Cornell Maritime Press, 1958.

Simmons, Walter J. *Lapstrake Boatbuilding, Vols. I and II.* Lincolnville Beach, ME: Duck Trap Press, 1993 and 1986.

_____. *Lines, Lofting and Half Models.* Lincolnville Beach, ME: Duck Trap Press, 1991.

Stelmok, Jerry, and Rollin Thurlow. *The Wood & Canvas Canoe.* Gardiner, ME: The Harpswell Press, 1987.

Steward, Robert M. *Boatbuilding Manual,* 4th Edition. Camden, ME: International Marine, 1994.

Spectre, Peter H., Editor. *The WoodenBoat Series: Painting & Varnishing.* WoodenBoat Publications, Inc., 1995.

_____. *The WoodenBoat Series: 10 Wooden Boats You Can Build.* WoodenBoat Publications, Inc., 1995.

Toss, Brion. *The Rigger's Apprentice,* 2nd Edition. Camden, ME: International Marine, 1992.

Witt, Glen L., and Ken Hankinson. *Boatbuilding with Plywood,* 3rd Edition. Bellflower, CA: Glen-L Marine, 1989.

Wittman, Rebecca. *Brightwork.* Camden, ME: International Marine, 1990.

WoodenBoat Editors. *The Directory of Wooden Boat Builders & Designers.* Brooklin, ME: WoodenBoat Publications, Inc., 1994.

Articles in *WoodenBoat*

Adhesives

Brown, Jim. "Wood & Epoxy." Parameters for success. WB No. 105, p. 94.

Buckley, Jennifer. "Holding Fast: Sonny Hodgdon on Glues." WB No. 59, p. 88.

Fraser, Aimé Ontario. "Goops and Goos." WB No. 92, p. 23.

_____. "Epoxy." WB No. 84, p. 48.

Jagels, Richard. "Gluing Wood: Adhering to Principles." WB No. 119, p. 98.

Ordering Information

Plans, books, and back issues listed on these pages may be ordered from The WoodenBoat Store, PO Box 78, Brooklin, Maine 04616.

For a free, up-to-date on-line index of *WoodenBoat* magazine, please visit www.woodenboat.com.

For future issues of *WoodenBoat* magazine, contact WoodenBoat Subscriptions, PO Box 78, Brooklin Maine 04616.

It's all on-line: www.woodenboat.com

WoodenBoat BOOKS

Featuring Books on Design, Boatbuilding, and Repair

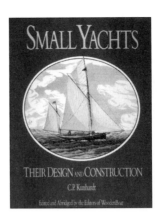

Small Yachts
by C.P. Kunhardt

In 1985 we revived this book, but it's been out of print for almost 20 years. *Small Yachts* is a fascinating look at a wonderful array of craft from the past: sharpies, canoe yawls, cutters, a variety of catboats, plus sneakboxes, bugeyes, and more. This is a careful reprint of the original 1891 book (less some technicals). Re-discover this jewel of a text. 288 pp., hardcover #0-937822-00-0 $30.00

100 Boat Designs Reviewed
Design Commentaries by the Experts

With this book in hand, you will hold the collective wisdom of the ages. Or at least the wisdom of the experts. A mountain of information has been culled from the best boat design reviews from WoodenBoat magazine. You'll spend hours pouring over a variety of boats, from rowing craft to powerboats, daysailers to cruising boats. The reviews are comprehensive and thorough. No once-over-lightly here. There is an analysis of the lines, construction plan, accommodation plan, plus recommendations for improvements. The scope of work includes designs by John Alden, Joel White, Henry Scheel, Howard Chapelle, S.S. Crocker, and many others. This is a wonderful book for boat dreamers. Study these plans, read these commentaries, go sailing in your mind. 264 pp., softcover, #0-937822-44-2 $24.95

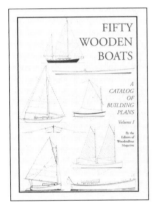

Fifty Wooden Boats

These popular books contain details usually found with study plans: hull dimensions, displacement, sail area, construction methods and the degree of boatbuilding skill needed to complete each project. Some of the 50 designs include John Alden's beloved Malabar II, Joel White's Nutshell Prams, Monroe's sharpie Egret, Fenwick Williams catboats, Gilmer's handsome Blue Moon yawl, and many more. See page 94 for a list of designs. 112 pp., softcover #0-937822-07-8 $12.95

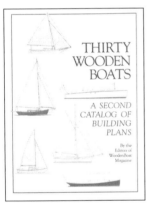

Thirty Wooden Boats

These 30 designs include: 6 powerboats, 6 daysailers, 11 cruising boats, 2 canoes, a kayak, and 4 small sailing/ pulling boats. Also included is an article by designer Joel White on understanding boat plans. See page 95 for a list of designs. 80 pp., softcover #0-937822-15-9 $12.95

Designs to Inspire
From *The Rudder* 1897 to 1942

Edited by Anne & Maynard Bray
A treasure trove of lines drawings faithfully reproduced from the original issues of *The Rudder*, improved only by Maynard's unique perspective, as he has written captions for each of the designs. Truly inspiring. 184 pp., softcover #0-937822-63-9 $24.95

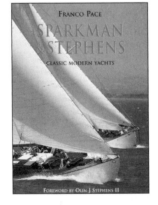

Sparkman & Stephens
Classic Modern Yachts

by Franco Pace
Sparkman & Stephens were undoubtedly one of the most successful and influential yacht designers in the history of modern yachting.

Formed as a result of the partnership between the Stephens brothers, Olin and Rod, and Drake Sparkman in the late 1920s, the breadth and dominance of their designs from 6, 8 and 12 metre boats to America's Cup yachts as well as a renowned fleet of ground breaking cruising and racing yachts, is quite remarkable. Dorade, Vim, Nyala, Columbia, Stormy Weather, Intrepid, Courageous: these are just some of the names which ring out in tribute to the brilliance of their creators. 160 pp., hardcover, #0-937822-75-2 $59.95

The Gaff Rig Handbook

by John Leather
The ultimate text covering the historical development and practical application of the gaff rig, via text, photographs, and very clear illustrations by Mr. Leather. A variety of craft is featured—catboats, sloops, cutters, yawls, ketches, and schooners. Plus there are sections on regional boats; New England and Nova Scotia, North West England, Denmark, and France. You'll get to see lots of handsome boats, and you'll understand why this rig has such staunch supporters.

240 pp., softcover
#0-937822-67-1 $29.95

Canoe Rig
The Essence and the Art

by Todd Bradshaw
Subtitled "Sailpower for Antique and Traditional Canoes," it will prepare you to examine how the wind might best move your boat. And it will open your eyes to sail and rig configurations

you may have never seen. All the information you need for building sails, spars, leeboards, centerboards, and more, is right here. The artwork is backed up by measurements, so you can create in the flesh what Todd has drawn.
265 pp., hardcover, #0-937822-57-4 $34.95

William Fife
Master of the Classic Yacht

by Franco Pace
What a combination: the vintage yachts of William Fife as photographed by Franco Pace, one of the top nautical photographers in the world. Hundreds of lush photographs, including full-page and full-spread shots. Nineteen different Fife boats are featured. Large format. 160 pp., hardcover, #0-937822-49-3 $69.95

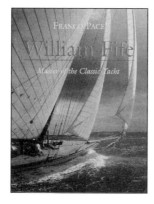

The Marisol Skiff

by Gifford Jackson
Even if one has no intention of building this or any other boat, this book will hold the readers' interest because of the huge amount of information in the plethora of drawings. One of the most complete plansets ever drawn, Gifford Jackson's Marisol Skiff is packed with interesting details including his two-part specialized trailer to make launching all the easier. Marisol (meaning sea & sun in Spanish) is a rugged daysailer... all 12'6" of her. Measured metrically, she is a v-bottomed dagger-boarder built in glue-lap-ply construction with sawn frames.
88 pp., hardcover, #0-937822-88-4 $19.95

Herreshoff and His Yachts

by Franco Pace
Nathanael Green Herreshoff was one of the giants of early 20th century yacht design -an innovator, a bold thinker but most of all a designer of graceful, beautiful racing yachts, many of which are still winning classic regattas today. He designed an impressive array of outstanding gaff riggers and Bermudian sloops for the America's Cup and remains one of the most revered yacht designers of the twentieth century.

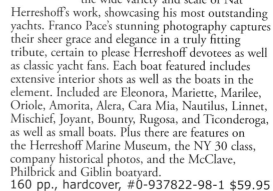

Having founded the Herreshoff Manufacturing Company with his (blind) brother John Brown Herreshoff in 1878, Nat designed a wide range of yachts, from the 162-foot Elenora, to the much beloved 16-foot Buzzard's Bay Boys Boat, known as 12½ (for its waterline length). Captain Nat was affectionately known as "The Wizard of Bristol" for his success and inventiveness in all aspects of boat design and manufacturing.

This book is a magnificent photographic collection celebrating the wide variety and scale of Nat Herreshoff's work, showcasing his most outstanding yachts. Franco Pace's stunning photography captures their sheer grace and elegance in a truly fitting tribute, certain to please Herreshoff devotees as well as classic yacht fans. Each boat featured includes extensive interior shots as well as the boats in the element. Included are Eleonora, Mariette, Marilee, Oriole, Amorita, Alera, Cara Mia, Nautilus, Linnet, Mischief, Joyant, Bounty, Rugosa, and Ticonderoga, as well as small boats. Plus there are features on the Herreshoff Marine Museum, the NY 30 class, company historical photos, and the McClave, Philbrick and Giblin boatyard.
160 pp., hardcover, #0-937822-98-1 $59.95

See More WoodenBoat Books
www.woodenboatbooks.com

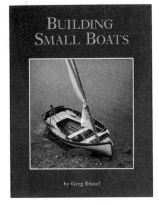

Building Small Boats

by Greg Rössel
The ideal book for the construction of boats under 25 feet in length, with a focus on two different traditional building methods; carvel (plank-on-frame) and lapstrake. It's perfect for folks looking to have some of the mysteries of the building process peeled away, or just boning-up on a good technique or two.
278 pp., hardcover
#0-937822-50-7 $39.95

BOOK OF THE YEAR!
Silver Medal Winner, from **Foreword** magazine

How to Build Glued-Lapstrake Wooden Boats

by John Brooks and Ruth Ann Hill
When you finish reading this book, you'll understand just what you need to do to build a terrific boat. A boat that is lightweight, forever appealing to the eye, a boat that doesn't leak and doesn't require much in the way of upkeep. And, because the book is clearly written and heavily illustrated with hundreds of drawings and hundreds of photographs, this lovely boat will look as though your stock in trade is indeed that of "boatbuilder". Read the book, and sharpen your tools because you'll just have sharpened your mind.
288 pp., hardcover
0-937822-58-2 $39.95

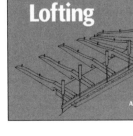

How to Build a Wooden Boat

by David C. "Bud" McIntosh
Illustrated by Sam Manning
Here is everything you need to know to construct a carvel planked cruising boat with no more than a set of plans, a pile of lumber, and determination. Written and illustrated by experienced boatbuilders, this book covers the entire process, from lofting to finishing out, setting up molds, lining off, ribbands, steaming and fitting frames, planking, pouring the keel, bulkheads and floorboards, decks, rudders, spars—the works. Originally published in 1988, we think it's Bud's very readable writing style combined with Sam Mannings wonderfully clear drawings that have made this such an endearing and enduring book.
254 pp., hardcover, #0-937822-10-8 $36.00

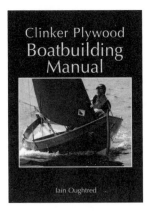

Clinker Plywood Boatbuilding Manual

by Iain Oughtred
Iain Oughtred is the well-known designer of elegant glued-lapstrake plywood boats, including the Acorn Skiffs, Gray Seal, Caledonia Yawl, Whilly Boat, and more. And, you may have noticed many of his designs in *WoodenBoat* magazine's Launchings column. With the book in hand, and a set of his plans, you can hardly go wrong. *Clinker Plywood Boatbuilding Manual* is encompassing enough to guide you through any lapstrake (aka Clinker) boatbuilding project. It covers tools and materials needed, lining off, setting up the building jig, planking, interior work, and fitting out. There are hundreds of drawings, hundreds of photos, and it's dosed liberally with Iain's pragmatic experience.
180 pp., softcover
#0-937822-61-2 $29.95

The New Cold-Molded Boatbuilding

by Reuel B. Parker
Ideally suited for the amateur builder wanting a good solid cruising boat, this is a complete, soup-to-nuts presentation of the cold-molding process, with chapters detailing every facet of construction—from choosing a design and setting up, through engine installation and wiring, to launching and sea trials. Parker has streamlined the cold-molding process to produce economical, sturdy boats.
320 pp., softcover
#0-937822-89-2 $19.95

Lofting

by Allan H. Vaitses
Lofting is the process of drawing lines of a boat full-size, to get the shapes and patterns needed for building. You take the numbers from the offset table, plot them on the floor, and then play connect the dots. Okay, it's not that simple. If it were, you wouldn't need the book. First published in the 1980s and out of print far too long, Lofting is that one-stop shopping for filling your void of this particular knowledge base. Because lofting is such a foundation element of boatbuilding, you really should understand how to do it. And while this topic has probably scared-off more folks from building than any other reason, fear not. You are in the best of care. Allan Vaitses, a boatman in the true sense of the word, had more than 50 years experience. He built over 200 boats, managed and owned boatyards, published over 40 articles in most of the major nautical magazines, holds design patents, and surveyed hundreds of boats. Sometimes there's no substitute for experience.
150 pp., softcover, 0-937822-55-8 $19.95

How to Build the Shellback Dinghy

by Eric Dow
Construct this 11' 2" dinghy following the step-by-step instructions of builder Eric Dow. The Shellback Dinghy is a modern classic that rows, tows, and sails beautifully. She has a traditional bow, a narrow rockered bottom, and a sweet transom that lifts well out of the water. Everything has been engineered with the amateur builder in mind. Study plans are featured in *Forty Wooden Boats*.
64 pp., softcover, #0-937822-27-2 $15.00

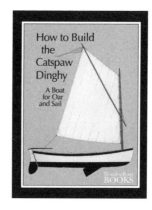

How to Build the Catspaw Dinghy

by the Editors of WoodenBoat
A detailed manual on the building of a superior rowing and sailing dinghy. A modified version (carvel instead of lapstrake planking) of the famous Herreshoff *Columbia* dinghy, this measures 12' 8", and makes an excellent project for the boatbuilder with intermediate skills. While offsets are included with this book, working from the plans is recommended. Study plans are featured in *Fifty Wooden Boats*.
32 pp., softcover, #0-937822-36-1 $9.95

How to Build the Haven 12 ½-Footer

by Maynard Bray
This is Joel White's keel/centerboard variation of the famous Herreshoff 12½. She's carvel planked, and each step in this unique process is carefully explained and illustrated. This book, in combination with detailed construction plans, provides a thorough guide for advanced amateurs. No lofting is required. Study plans are featured in *Thirty Wooden Boats*.
64 pp., softcover, #0-937822-13-2 $15.00

Building the Nutshell Pram

by Maynard Bray
A step-by-step construction manual for this very popular Joel White design, for oar and sail. Part of the popularity is due to the ease of construction, especially the bow. This instruction book is beneficial for anyone who wishes to understand how easy (or hard) building this pram really is. Study plans are featured in *Fifty Wooden Boats*. 32 pp., softcover
#0-937822-11-6 $9.95

Featherweight Boatbuilding

by Henry "Mac" McCarthy
It is Mac's mission to open your eyes to the natural beauty around you. He does so by providing this "course" to create and use an ideal double-paddle canoe. The Wee Lassie is practical and beautiful, lightweight and strong, and will carry you to waterways that are inaccessible in most boats. Mac draws on years of experience teaching hundreds of people in his shop, and at our WoodenBoat School in Brooklin, Maine. The Wee Lassie is strip-built, an especially forgiving building technique for the first-time builder. This book contains everything you need to build two different sized Wee Lassies—step-by-step photographs, clear easy to follow text, diagrams, plans—and inspiration. On top of that, plans and instructions for building a double-paddle, as wells as how to do the caning of the seat are included.
96 pp., softcover, #0-937822-39-6 $19.95

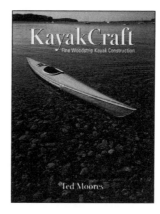

KayakCraft

Fine Woodstrip Kayak Construction

by Ted Moores
When you skim through *KayakCraft* two things are immediately apparent; the simple elegance of Steve Killing's proven designs, and the carefully detailed and documented processes of Ted Moores, a builder and teacher whose forté is passing on his ability to make exquisite small craft. Even if you have built a strip canoe, you'll want this book for the designs as well as the additional techniques for making the cockpit coaming, hatches, and decking. While the popular 17' Endeavour kayak is the boat used throughout the book, *KayakCraft* also gives you lines and offsets for three other Steve Killing designed kayaks: a 14' sport kayak, a 16' 6" touring kayak, and a 20' 6" tandem kayak. And, strip-building is a very forgiving technique because the cost of ruining a piece of skinny stripwood is minimal. 185 pp., softcover
#0-937822-56-6 $19.95

Traditional Boatbuilding Made Easy
Building Heidi
by Richard Kolin

This is wooden boatbuilding at its most pleasurable—a 12' skiff done in the traditional manner—solid planking, copper clench nails, bronze fittings, the aroma of cedar planking, turps, and penetrating oils. Rich's clear drawings, including isometrics, and friendly text make this the ideal way to get into traditional construction.

86 pp., softcover
#0-937822-40-X $19.95

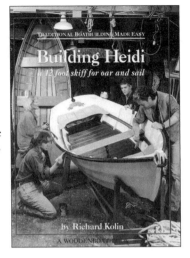

Traditional Boatbuilding Made Easy
Building Catherine
a 14 foot pulling boat in the whitehall tradition

by Richard Kolin

Described as a cross between two of our most popular designs, Joel White's Catspaw Dinghy, and Iain Oughtred's Acorn Skiff, the Catherine is everything a traditional boat should be, except overly complex to build. It's traditional lapstrake planked, tons of drawings, and clear step-by-step procedures.

98 pp., softcover
#0-937822-62-0 $19.95

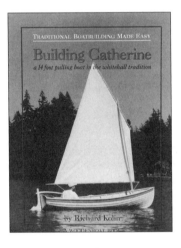

Boatbuilding Down East
How Lobsterboats are Built

by Royal Lowell

We are pleased to bring this book back into print. Written by Royal Lowell, it features many of his lobsterboat designs, and is truly a builder's guide for traditional lobsterboats.

Well illustrated, the book includes lines for several boats (no offsets) including a 36-foot lobsterboat, a 32-foot sport cruiser, and a 26-foot sport fisherman. If you too have fallen in love with the lines of lobsterboats, you will be especially pleased to have this book, as there is so little published on the type. The book content is succinctly put into perspective for us in the foreword, written by noted marine historian Maynard Bray.

This edition is true to the original book, although there is the addition of listing of all of Royal Lowell's designs.

Cover artwork is an acrylic by noted marine artist R.B. Dance. He is known for his painstakingly accurate painting, especially when it comes to lobsterboats.

190 pp., hardcover, #0-937822-73-6 $29.95

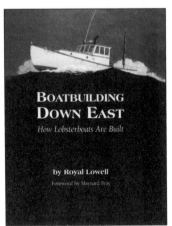

The Making of Tom Cat
A Fathom Wide by Two-Plus Fathoms Long
by William Garden

You'll enjoy this… part story, part boatbuilding manual of a small, beetle-cat-like boat, from a legendary designer with probably more of his creations built than any other person. You'll find out not only how the boat is built, but also how the design came to be from someone with a (long!) lifetime of fooling around with boats. As told from

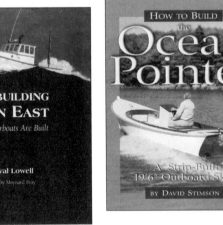

Toad's Landing, on an island off British Columbia, it becomes quite apparent that whimsy and fun are not limited to young boys and girls.

The first thing you may notice about Tom Cat is the handsome cuddy. The next thing to realize is she is constructed with a combination of the traditional-plank-on-frame (carvel) and modern-epoxy for the seams. The result is a rugged boat which doesn't require the swelling of planks, or the recaulking of seams in the years to come. If you are just too pure a traditionalist for epoxy, of course you can plank and caulk.

52 pp., hardcover
#0-937822-78-7 $17.95

How to Build the Ocean Pointer
A Strip-built 19'6" Outboard Skiff

by David Stimson

Based on the Alton Wallace 18' round-bilged outboard skiff known as the West Pointer, the Ocean Pointer is a bit larger, and a significantly drier boat with a sweeping sheer, able to accommodate a 25-75 hp outboard.

Designer/builder David Stimson created this boat to be strip-built (narrow pieces of wood), which is an especially forgiving building method for the less experienced builder.

This book provides step-by-step instructions on the building process so the reader will easily be able to determine if this is their ideal craft, and if so inclined, have at it. She'll move nicely through the water, and between that sheer and the aft tumblehome, she has a shape you'll never tire of.

57 pp., softcover, #0-937822-72-8 $17.95

Painting & Varnishing

No matter the standard of finish—utilitarian through show quality and anything in between—the keys to success are a well-conceived plan of action, the correct choice of tools and materials, a careful preparation of the surface, proper application of the coating, and a "feel" for what you are doing. This book contains twenty-four articles from *WoodenBoat* magazine, including: Quick Steps to Spring Painting; Paint Adhesion; The Wood/Paint Interface: Will It Stick?; Mildew, and Lots of It!; Painting for Longevity; Painting for Decoration; Rolling and Tipping; Paintbrush Care; For Her Name's Sake; Name in Gold, Hail in Black; The Fine Art of Stripping Paint; Taking It Off with Chemical Strippers; Scrapers; and more.
 146 pp., softcover
#0-937822-33-7 $24.95

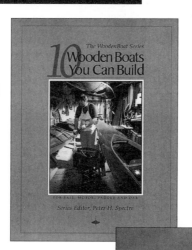

10 Wooden Boats You Can Build

For Sail, Power, Oar and Paddle
The beauty of this book is that the construction bugs have already been worked out of the designs. Plans, step-by-step instructions, materials lists, clear photographs, and detailed diagrams are included. Follow the building process for a variety of designs: a Herreshoff Daysailer, a Lapstrake Plywood Runabout, a Norwegian Pram, a Strip-Built Double-Paddle Canoe, a Cold-Molded Dinghy, a Bateau, and a Double-Paddle Lapstrake Sailing Canoe.
196 pp., softcover
#0-937822-34-5 $24.95

Frame, Stem & Keel Repair

The keel, stem, and frames are the very core of wooden boat construction, the elements that provide shape and strength to the structure. They are analogous to the sill, joists, rafters, and framing of a house. If they have integrity, the structure has integrity. If they don't, they must be fixed or the structure will not survive. Here is practical advice from the experts. In most cases, they make their points by reviewing a specific project step-by-step, describing why they did what they did, and how they did it. Coverage includes: Why Bent Frames Break, and How to Fix Them; Bending Wood; An Unpressured Approach to Steaming; A Steam Box Primer; A Steam Box Scrapbook; Reframing a Yacht; Stem, Transom, and Frame Repairs for a 12 1/2 footer; Extending the Life of a St. Lawrence Skiff; Removing Tension in New Frames; Making Laminated Frames; An Alternative Frame-Repair Technique, and more.
133 pp., softcover
#0-937822-42-6 $24.95

Planking & Fastening

Perhaps the most satisfying task in wooden boat building is planking, as this is the point when all the planning that went into the boat bears fruit. Finally, all the elements are here—the flowing lines, the lovely sheer, the enclosed space. Now it looks like a boat. Gathered here is the information necessary for preparing to plank, clamping the planks in place, fastening the planks to the structure, and finishing off. The advice is based on actual projects, some large, some small; the advisors are all expert wooden boatbuilders. This book is a gold mine of information that will help and encourage readers with the building of a new boat or the repair of an old one. Chapters include: Lining off Planking; Plank Curvature; A Drying Rack for Planking Stock; The Mechanics of Fastening Wood; A Close Look at Wood Screws; Bungs A Few Pointers; Making and Setting Bungs; Clamps in the Boatshop; A Wooden Clamp You Can Build Yourself; Small Clamps for Small Boats; Lining, Spiling, and Geting Out a Plank; Carvel Planking Tips from a Professional; Planking the Morgan; Edge-Setting Planks; Wedge-Seam Construction, and more. 170 pp., softcover
0-937822-41-8 $24.95

25 Woodworking Projects

For Small and Large Boats
Packed wtih projects for the novice and expert. Here are some of the best woodworking projects shown in WoodenBoat magazine. They range from a simple bailer, to a stunning ship's wheel. And in between are oars, single and double-bladed paddles, louvered doors, an icebox, a skylight, hollow spars, and much more. With plenty of photos and drawings, the step-by-step processes described will help ensure each project's success as well as provide the personal satisfaction of having completed it yourself.
198 pp., softcover
#0-937822-46-9 $22.95

Fifty Wooden Boats
by the Editors of WoodenBoat

This popular book contains details usually found with study plans: hull dimensions, displacement, sail area, construction methods, and the degree of skill needed to complete each project. There are drawings that identify the parts of a wooden boat, a guide for the selection of various woods, and an article on reading boat plans.
112 pp., illus., softcover #325-060
Ship Wt. 1 lb $12.95

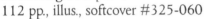

18'3" Sloop, O-Boat, by John G. Alden

Study Plans Catalogs

Thirty Wooden Boats
by the Editors of WoodenBoat

More study plans selected by the Editors of *WoodenBoat.*
This volume describes designs added to our collection
since the publication of *Fifty Wooden Boats.* Although the
style remains much the same, all the designs are new
offerings, and range from a 7′ 10″ tender to a 37′ 3″ yawl.
80 pp., illus., softcover
#325-061 Ship Wt. ½ lb **$12.95**

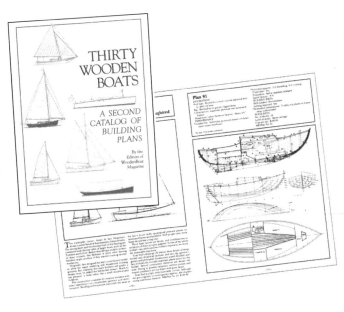

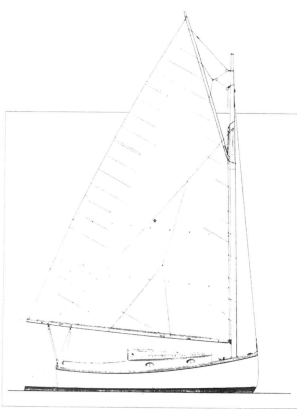

20′ Plywood Catboat, Madam Tirza, by Charles Wittholz

WoodenBoat Plans Policies

This catalog has been designed to inform and educate readers and prospective builders. While all information has been obtained from reliable sources and we believe it to be accurate, NO WARRANTY CAN BE MADE OR SHOULD BE IMPLIED with respect to this catalog's contents. Readers are urged to rely on their own good sense and personal experience when considering any design for reasons of performance or ease of construction.

While all care has been taken with each set of plans offered, the designer and WoodenBoat DISCLAIM ALL LIABILITY for loss or injury to property or person which might occur while using these boats, including loss due to careless handling or sailing of the boat under conditions beyond its reasonable limits. We also DISCLAIM ALL LIABILITY for boats built of inferior materials, to substandard workmanship, or to specifications or construction methods other than those suggested by the designer. Plans buyers who wish to modify a design IN ANY WAY are cautioned to do so only under the guidance of a competent naval architect.

Note: Plans are sold with the understanding that one boat only may be built from each set. If you wish to build more than one boat, please write for royalty terms. Plans may not be reproduced in any form, or by electronic or mechanical means, without permission.

*General Notes on Designs

Particulars: For purposes of this catalog, LOA (length overall) is equivalent to LOD (length on deck).

Performance section: WoodenBoat's comments concerning the type of waters a boat is suited for, as well as a vessel's intended capacity (number of persons), are based on the boat being used by experienced people in favorable wind and sea conditions. Owners are advised to check U.S. Coast Guard capacity regulations, where applicable.

Building Data section: Information regarding alternative construction methods for a design means only that the hull shape would lend itself to these alternative methods. Unless otherwise noted, plans do not include details for modified construction and builders must rely on their own resources.